Due Diligence

DUE DILIGENCE

Planning, Questions, Issues

Gordon Bing

**Westport, Connecticut
London**

Library of Congress Cataloging-in-Publication Data

Bing, Gordon.
   Due diligence : planning, questions, issues / Gordon Bing.
      p. cm.
   Updates: Due diligence techniques and analysis. 1996.
   Includes bibliographical references and index.
   ISBN 978–0–313–34540–1 (alk. paper)
1. Business enterprises—Purchasing—Handbooks, manuals, etc. 2. Sale of business
enterprises—Handbooks, manuals, etc. 3. Investment analysis—Handbooks, manuals, etc.
4. Disclosure of information—Handbooks, manuals, etc. I. Bing, Gordon. Due diligence
techniques and analysis. II. Title.
HD1393.25.B56 2008
658.1′62—dc22   2007038550

British Library Cataloguing in Publication Data is available.

Library of Congress Catalog Card Number: 2007038550

First published in 2008

Praeger Publishers, 88 Post Road West, Westport, CT 06881
An imprint of Greenwood Publishing Group, Inc.
www.praeger.com

Printed in the United States of America

The paper used in this book complies with the
Permanent Paper Standard issued by the National
Information Standards Organization (Z39.48–1984).

10 9 8 7 6 5 4 3 2 1

Contents

Preface   xiii

1. Getting Started: Basic Information   1

2. Preliminary Critical Information   7

3. Key Early Issues and Alarms   11

4. Ownership and Capital Structure   17

5. Directors and Governance   21

6. Management   25

7. Products and Services   31

8. R&D and Technology   35

9. Markets and Customers   39

10. Competition   43

11. Marketing, Selling, and Distribution   47

12. Pricing   51

13. Advertising   55

14. Public and Investor Relations   57

15. Manufacturing   61

16. Purchasing and Outsourcing   67

17. Human Resources and Employees   71

18. Union Issues   77

19. Employee Compensation and Benefits   81

20. Retirement Plans, 401(k)s, and ESOPs   85

21. Culture of the Business   89

22. Legal and Regulatory Issues   93

23. Government Business, Lobbying, and Politics   99

24. Information Systems   105

25. Internet   109

26. Budgets   111

27. Planning   113

28. Insurance and Bonding   115

29. Environment and Safety Issues   119

30. Debt, Banks, and Financial Institutions   123

31. Investments, Hedging, and Derivatives   127

32. Cash and Cash Management   131

33. Accounting: General Questions   135

34. Accounting Policies   139

35. Accounts and Notes Receivable   143

36. Taxes   147

37. Inventory   151

38. Fixed and Other Assets   155

39. Liabilities   159

40. Cost of Sales and Gross Profit   163

41. Selling and General and Administrative Expenses (SG&A)   165

42. Income Recognition and Backlog   167

43. Intracompany Transactions   171

44. Real Estate   175

45. Investment Questions and Issues   179

46. Off–Balance Sheet Items   183

47. Assets and Liabilities Excluded   187

48. Financial Ratios and Trends   191

49. Warning Signs   195

50. Outrageous Improprieties   197

Index   199

Preface

This is a book for those seeking to study an entire business or segments of a business. It describes a systematic approach, techniques, the questions to ask, the documents to review, and issues to explore. The investigative process consists of three general categories of activity: information gathering, evaluation including quantification, and conclusions leading to decisions. Document review and questions are the first steps in the process. The validity of the decisions is influenced by both the questions asked and if all pertinent questions were asked. Knowing what questions to ask, and which documents to review, is the foundation of the due diligence process. After all information is obtained, and the positive and negative aspects of the business are quantified, intelligent conclusions and decisions are possible.

The primary and usual purpose of due diligence is to verify that the business is in the condition the investor believed it was in while considering or reaching a preliminary agreement. This confirmation activity includes a search for undisclosed liabilities and problems and an overall understanding of the business. An investor may have other secondary objectives, such as: discovering undervalued assets, identifying high-potential employees, finding synergistic opportunities, obtaining information to plan a transition of ownership, and information for new management to "hit the ground running." All of these are valuable objectives, but the primary purpose will remain confirmation of the assumed condition of the business and a search for negative conditions.

While this book is primarily for the conduct of due diligence prior to an acquisition or merger, and as a basis for those wishing to construct their own industry-specific checklists, there are others who will find it an invaluable reference book:

1. Newly appointed executives attempting to learn what they are managing.
2. Executives seeking understanding of problems, departments, or divisions.
3. Those involved in lending to businesses.
4. Venture capitalists.
5. Appraisers.
6. Attorneys arguing there was either adequate or inadequate due diligence.
7. Business students involved in case studies or reports on a business.
8. Individuals evaluating a company when offered a new position.
9. Any organization or individuals involved in preparation of private placement memorandums or other security offerings.

Whoever is the user and for whatever purpose, the questions will be a first step in discovering the information needed.

There are no perfect businesses, and all are a combination of desirable attributes as well as of aspects needing improvement or to be discarded. In a due diligence study, you verify the positive features of the business that prompted the study and pursue a search for defects and unknown aspects. As you accumulate information, a continuous process of quantification should occur to avoid giving excessive value to positive factors or becoming overly alarmed about the negatives. Attempting to quantify factors is not a precise process, but one requiring business judgment, an open mind, and a willingness to put forth the effort. In practice, quantification may be comprehensive and prove invaluable or cursory, depending on the ability and personal motivation of those reviewing the data.

At the start of each chapter is a commentary on the subjects and issues covered. The commentary contains observations and may alert investigators to potential problems requiring extra attention. The questions posed in the book assume the user has business experience and a good level of sophistication. It also assumes investigators will know when professionals with special expertise should be retained. Explanations of the purpose of individual questions are not presented, since for most users such is unnecessary. Regardless, every question has a purpose, but not for every business. There is also no attempt to be judgmental either by posing a question or in its phrasing. Every due diligence investigation is unique and must be tailored to the specific situation, taking into consideration all relevant factors: size of the transaction, cost, number of locations, risks, staff available, etc. Procedures and methods for conducting due diligence studies also tend to evolve from a buyer's experience and hopefully improve with each investigation.

While most of the subjects are in the form of questions, their purpose is to identify a subject that may need further study, can be put to rest, or is irrelevant. A perceptive investigator will make decisions based on the responses and decide to pursue a subject or move on to the next. The skill and perceptiveness of those conducting the study is an indispensable factor in its quality.

A fundamental problem when studying and investigating a business is the plethora of information obtained, but not sorted, to identify the most essential. The quantity of information is a partial result of not knowing in advance where every problem may lie, forcing a review of all aspects of the business. Yet excessive information can obscure important data buried in stacks of data. Therefore, the best solution starts with a systematic study, involving comprehensive checklists containing pertinent questions and lists of documents for review. With this book, anyone can construct his or her own checklist for use in evaluation of businesses or segments of a business. When constructing a checklist utilizing questions found in this book, it will become readily apparent that a much shorter list will be possible, since many questions will be irrelevant for the business under study. Questions will have to be added to cover subjects unique to a specific industry. The book is structured with categories of questions for ready reference and the deletion of those not appropriate for an industry or specific business. Regardless of how well constructed the checklist is, its value will be realized only if the information gathered is systematically preserved and actually reviewed by personnel with the ability to evaluate the data.

Most regrettable acquisitions constitute due diligence failures. There is no better illustration of this principle than the disastrous acquisition of Dresser Industries by Halliburton. The presence of asbestos claim exposure in a small subsidiary and accusations of corrupt foreign practices—which could have been exposed if comprehensive due diligence had been conducted—would have saved Halliburton billions of dollars. While success or failure relative to acquisitions and mergers may have varying definitions, all evidence indicates the majority fail if the definition of success is meeting pre-acquisition financial projections. Of course, the Halliburton affair is only one of hundreds of failures that occurred in the past decade, a decade that properly may be described as "The Golden Age of Corporate Deceit." The business press is replete with stories of business failure, loan defaults, public offerings in which the price soon collapsed, and investment scandals with the losers saying, "I wish I had known."

The Halliburton debacle illustrates two other major facts relevant to due diligence: reliance solely upon audited financial statements, information from a few senior executives, and information prepared by intermediaries is a high-risk mistake. The motivation of sellers and their representatives who have a significant financial interest in the outcome may color information presented or withheld and should continually remind investors to be wary. The other problem is that, within a corporation that owns or controls multiple business units, there may be wide variations as to how each conducts business, and each unit should receive full due diligence attention. Senior management may not even be aware of serious problems lurking in subsidiaries (see Chapter 50, "Outrageous Improprieties").

Due diligence is successful when defects and problems are discovered early enough for the deal to be renegotiated or avoided entirely. Another form of success is confirming the business is as represented and no surprises emerge after closing. On the other hand, due diligence is a failure when the investor is belatedly surprised by information that, if known before closing, would have postponed or cancelled the closing. Other common causes of failure in addition to those in the above paragraph are: limited competence of those conducting the study, inadequate time, a cursory study because of executive hubris, and overreliance on a seller's oral responses. All of the causes of failure listed constitute a reminder of what to avoid.

Many of the questions may be viewed as simple common sense. Others may be considered variations of basic questions commonly appearing in other checklists, but many critical questions refer to issues that first surfaced during the past decade, conceived by ingenious executives. These were techniques for manipulating income, self-enrichment, and deceiving investors, customers, and employees. The questions in this book should alert investigators conducting due diligence to the presence of old improprieties, but no one should underestimate the ability of amoral executives to conceive and engage in clever, new brazen schemes. A list of some of the more egregious schemes of the past 10 years appears in the last chapter as a reminder of how many were deceived and how many years had passed before exposure. Systematic due diligence can create alarms indicating further investigation of unorthodox activities is warranted.

Note: Throughout the book, the terms "buyer" or "investor" and "seller" are used, although in not all cases do the terms represent the intention of the parties. "Buyer" and "investor" are used to indicate the party conducting the due diligence investigation, and "seller" is the party being studied.

CHAPTER 1
Getting Started:
Basic Information

Due diligence is normally conducted during the period after reaching a preliminary agreement and before signing a binding contract. It is also essential preparation for private placement memorandums and documents involving the issuance of securities. The final contract's terms may be modified or terminated depending upon the results of the due diligence. The duration of the period for due diligence is usually negotiated by the parties and constitutes a critical factor in planning and organizing the program. Too short a period may make adequate investigation impossible, but unlimited time may result in a poorly organized program and the intrusion of unanticipated events, causing one or both parties to have second thoughts.

Early in planning a due diligence investigation, an investor is confronted with the due diligence dilemma, a dilemma requiring difficult choices for which there are no precise guidelines. The dilemma poses the basic question of how much due diligence is enough. An investor wants to know everything possible about the business and particularly significant problems or defects, but is limited by personnel, cost, time and other constraints. An investor must survey his resources and, based on available information, deploy the resources. It is unlikely that an investor will learn everything about a business with due diligence, nor is it necessary to learn everything. An investor must decide what information is essential and eventually make a judgment decision that enough has been obtained to proceed, while accepting the fact that more could be learned. Emphasis will initially be on suspected problem areas, but as the investigation continues, new subjects for intense investigation may emerge. The chance of discovery of concealed or undisclosed problems will increase with systematic use of questions presented by experienced and perceptive investigators.

Both the investor and the seller must cooperate and organize to accomplish the program in the agreed period of time. Investor personnel will plan and manage the entire program, decide who will participate, identify data and documents to be obtained, accumulate and store the information, and evaluate the business. The seller must select and notify those in the organization responsible for meeting with investor representatives and obtaining whatever information or documents are requested. In most cases, the seller is obligated to provide all information and data requested but no more, making it incumbent upon the investor to conduct an extremely comprehensive study of the business.

A system for the orderly flow of seller information and access must be promptly established. An early discussion is necessary between the investor and seller's executives who are directly involved in the due diligence study, in order to agree upon procedures that will contribute to an efficient study. A working relationship can resolve unanticipated conflicts and address the concerns of both parties. However, refusals or unexplained long delays in providing data or access will lead an investor to assume negative information is being withheld. This may very well be the case. Whenever there is a suspicion of negative information being withheld, an investor must react by becoming all the more determined to obtain the data.

Secrecy or confidential information agreements are commonly signed at the request of a potential seller, restricting the investor's use of information and proscribing penalties for violation of the agreements. These are signed at the start of discussions prior to a preliminary agreement, but supplementary agreements often become necessary, describing in more detail how due diligence will be conducted. A contentious issue frequently exists as to about what and when the investor may interview seller employees, vendors, and customers. A clear understanding must exist on the conduct of due diligence that permits the investor to obtain whatever information he believes is necessary, yet respects the desire of the seller for secrecy and concerns on how information gained could be used if no transaction occurs.

An essential part of due diligence preparation is the establishment of a system and central location for the data, documents, reports, and observations accumulated during the study. The voluminous quantity of material acquired during a study must be organized for ready reference and retention. The source of every document should be recorded, and control should be maintained over documents temporarily not in the central location. The material should also be a point of reference in the transition after the transaction is complete. Strict control over all material accumulated will aid in its orderly evaluation and permit ready reference as negotiations continue, are suspended, or are terminated. Frequently, the parties fail to reach a final agreement but at a later date resume negotiations, necessitating reference to the files. Another critical factor is that almost all secrecy agreements require close control of the material provided and the return of all such material in the event the transaction does not occur.

Internal coordination within the buyer's organization is also essential. Frequently, negotiations and due diligence activity are conducted by those skilled in these matters, but they are not the executives responsible for overseeing the business once acquired. It is advisable to have the operational executives involved as much as possible to review data, express their opinions, and gain their full support. The executive responsible for the acquisition may be eager to "get another notch on his gun," but the operations executive is concerned with his ability to run the business successfully and how it could affect his career.

To start and conduct a comprehensive due diligence program, the investor must select an executive to be responsible for the entire program and interface with the seller. Someone must be in charge, and this individual should have stature and a broad understanding of business. Thorough knowledge of business practices and the ability to perceive or suspect negative features of the business under study will be a major factor in the efficacy of the due diligence. The individual in charge must decide upon who will assist in the study. The composition of the team will depend upon a number of factors: the size of the business under study and the number of locations, the level of technology to be evaluated, the availability of personnel, the time constraints for completion, the depth of study believed necessary, and the amount the investor is willing to spend on due diligence. Team members may include investor employees, auditors, consultants, and investment bankers. Whoever is involved, their assignments must be clear and defined with strict time limits.

If the business to be studied is not a complete business, including all assets, liabilities, and employees, then an understanding must be reached to define the business. Joint ventures, subsidiaries, divisions, product lines, spin-offs and other divestitures from parent companies are seldom complete stand-alone businesses. Facilities may be shared with the seller's retained business, management may overlap, and financial and professional services and cash management may be provided by the seller or others. The due diligence investigators may find an important part of their task is to define exactly what is and is not to be acquired. They also may assist in the planning of the transition and how necessary functions not acquired will be replaced. Intracompany transactions of all types, including pricing, management fees, and overhead allocations, require careful study. The seller may not even be aware of the actual profitability of the business for sale. The quality of the financial statements may become an issue, with the investor finding the business is much better or worse than represented (see Chapter 47, "Assets and Liabilities Excluded").

After the investor selects his team and a working relationship is established with the seller, a foundation should exist from which to plan and conduct the due diligence program.

QUESTIONS AND PROCEDURES

1. Date when due diligence study commences?
2. Date when study must be complete?
3. Name of person responsible for managing, organizing, and selecting participants and approving expenditures incurred during the study. Will this person be the principal contact with the seller?
4. Identify employees, auditors, consultants, or retained organizations participating in the study. What will be their role and estimated cost? Will any benefit financially if the investment is made?
5. Obtain the legal name of the business. Does it commonly operate under shorter or different names?
6. Obtain the address, telephone number, e-mail addresses, and fax number of the business headquarters and/or the owner.
7. Obtain the names, titles, telephone numbers, e-mail addresses, and fax numbers of the seller's principals involved in negotiating the transaction.
8. Who will be the seller's primary contact during due diligence?
9. Has a comprehensive understanding been reached as to access to the seller's records, executives, customers, etc.?
10. Have the names, titles, telephone numbers, e-mail addresses, and fax numbers of seller executives and others authorized to provide information for the due diligence study been obtained?
11. What is the purpose and objectives of this due diligence study? In addition to verifying the condition of the business, are there other objectives, such as gathering data for a post-acquisition transition or searching for synergistic assets to justify the price?

12. Identify investor personnel to be involved in evaluating information and documents accumulated. Has one central location been established for the data and documents accumulated?

13. Has a confidentiality or secrecy agreement been signed? If yes:

    a) Who is responsible for compliance during due diligence?

    b) Who will be responsible for compliance if no transaction occurs?

14. What degree of secrecy must be maintained throughout the study with the seller's employees, customers, and competitors?

15. Are there any restrictions excluding subjects or individuals from the study?

16. If the seller has set up a "war room" in which all data is placed in one room and made available to interested qualified investors, what are the rules for access and obtaining data not available in the room?

17. What secrecy must be maintained within the investor's organization?

18. How will coordination be maintained between those involved in negotiating the transaction, those conducting due diligence, and those responsible for operations after the transaction?

19. Is it clearly understood as to what is being acquired and the precise nature of all assets, liabilities, and functions of the business to be studied? Identify all assets, liabilities, or functions to be retained by the seller.

CHAPTER 2
Preliminary Critical Information

Organized and systematic due diligence usually commences after the conclusion of some preliminary agreement or in the preparation of documents for the issuance of securities. At this point, the investor will possess a substantial amount of information relative to the seller, and the first step is to accumulate this data. By doing so, requests for data already in hand are avoided, and it is possible to determine what is missing. Some of the missing data can be readily secured from public sources, but most must be obtained directly from the seller.

The preliminary critical information will enable the investor to plan the due diligence program. The scope, time objectives for the study, personnel involved, professionals to be employed, and problem areas requiring extra attention all become part of the overall plan. Consultations with investor executives and those participating in negotiations can identify the desirable aspects of the business that made it attractive, as well as any suspected problems. It is quite normal in negotiations for the seller to emphasize favorable attributes and gloss over the problems. Buyers eager to conclude an agreement tend to accept a seller's presentations, but with the expectation that due diligence will produce an objective view. During due diligence, the positive and negative features should be studied equally, with a degree of skepticism but a goal of objectivity. Skepticism is particularly warranted if the buyer relied heavily on a "book" of information or a "war room" of data prepared by the seller's representatives.

All of the information and documents referred to in this section will eventually be acquired during the course of the due diligence study. However, as many as possible should be obtained prior to in-depth

questioning of the business's executives and employees. This preliminary information is primarily for the purpose of enabling the buyer to
plan the due diligence program. With this information, the study can
be efficiently planned, but recognizing that during a comprehensive
study additional documents will be obtained or reviewed. This is only
a start.

**The first step is to gather all the information and documents
already accumulated relative to the seller and set up a system for
its storage and preservation.**

Documents and public information:

1. Search the Internet for all information on the business.
2. All SEC filings. Available over the Internet at http://www.SEC.gov.
3. Industry trade publications.
4. Newspaper file (*Wall Street Journal*).
5. Reports from any security analysts on the business or industry.
6. Organization records, charter, bylaws from Secretary of State.
7. Uniform commercial code filings with Secretary of State.
8. *Who Owns Whom* (Reference book).
9. *Wards Business Directory* (Reference book).
10. *Directory of Corporate Affiliations* (Reference book).

Documents and information to request from seller:

1. Five years of annual financial statements.
2. Five years of tax returns.
3. Monthly financial statements since last annual statement.
4. Annual reports and proxy statements for past five years.
5. Descriptive brochures describing seller.
6. An organization chart with key personnel and reporting relationships.
7. Charter and bylaws and certificate of incorporation.
8. Minute books for five years.
9. Stock record books.

QUESTIONS AND PROCEDURES

1. What is the business's history? Obtain copies of any prepared histories of
   the business if such have been written. Who founded the business and

when? List significant events or milestones such as acquisitions, owner-ship changes, new products or services, and major business policy changes.

2. If a corporation, when was the business incorporated? Where is it incor-porated today?

3. If not a corporation, what is its legal structure?

4. List all subsidiaries, percent of ownership, names of directors, officers, managers, addresses, and the primary business activities.

5. List all divisions, names of managers, addresses, and primary business activities.

6. List all joint ventures and partnerships with names of directors, manag-ers, percentages of ownership, addresses, and primary business activity.

7. List all minority investments in operating businesses or business ven-tures with percentages of ownership, addresses, primary business activity, and history of the investment.

8. List the states and countries in which business is conducted. Is it properly licensed and in good standing in each?

9. Request or prepare a corporate organization chart showing the organiza-tion's legal relationship to each subsidiary, division, joint venture, part-nership, or minority investment.

10. Identify all professionals, such as attorneys, investment bankers, account-ants, consultants, finders, actuaries, etc., who may be involved, and claim compensation for services associated with this transaction. What are their estimated fees? Are any fees in dispute or expected to be controversial.

11. A list of all locations of the business and their functions and addresses.

CHAPTER 3
Key Early
Issues and Alarms

Early on in the investigative process, there may emerge issues and conditions of such importance that an investor will conclude it necessary to either modify his position or not proceed further. Conditions and issues may have been known but not quantified, suspected, or concealed, but are now identified and require prompt attention. Those involved in negotiating a preliminary agreement should have more than a superficial knowledge of the business and can recommend areas for close scrutiny, but the unknowns must be ferreted out. The negotiating process involves an element of "selling," with potential problems often glossed over or bypassed in an effort to reach an agreement. Negotiators tend to be focused on the "big picture," and issues thought to be of secondary importance are minimized or ignored. The problems are left for due diligence investigators to discover and evaluate.

The key questions in this chapter constitute a system of alarms. An alarm should sound in the minds of investigators when the response to any question is bad news, indicates a lack of knowledge of the subject, or reveals a potential problem requiring a prompt in-depth investigation. Early identification of significant issues or conditions allows those conducting the study to focus quickly on the key issues and prioritize others. If a major negative issue or condition not previously disclosed is found to exist, the buyer may attempt to renegotiate or walk away without devoting more time and money to due diligence. Fortunately, most of the conditions upon investigation will prove to be of minor significance or easily explained, but an investor must know either way.

The questions enable those planning a study to avoid inapplicable subjects. There will always be such a large amount of pertinent documents and issues that confining the study to the relevant is essential. Every study must be planned and work assignments made. Depending upon the size, complexity, and number of locations of the seller, the personnel required may range from one person to a large team involving many professionals. With possible time constraints and associated costs, it is prudent to decide at the first stage on subjects to be avoided or for cursory review. A business in an office building requires little environmental attention. A business free of uninsured lawsuits need not employ attorneys to review litigation. Due diligence will never be without cost, but wasteful expenditures can be avoided with careful planning.

Financial reports are only a snapshot of the financial condition of the business at some past point in time. They record history with limited value in predicting the future in a rapidly changing world. The individual line items are summaries that often obscure important information. Great reliance was probably placed on the seller's statements by the negotiators, but they should only be a starting point for those conducting due diligence. Excessive reliance on financial reports as an indication of the future is undoubtedly a prime cause of buyer mistakes.

These questions are designed as alarms to assist the buyer by quickly identifying critical issues. Most of the questions are repeated and elaborated upon in later sections of the book. There are also hundreds of other questions that may appear to be unimportant or even irrelevant at this early stage, but their answers emerge as "deal killers" nonetheless. This chapter provides an overview of the business, but should not be construed as an abbreviated due diligence checklist or program. One never knows until a question is asked as to its importance, and there are hundreds of other questions to ask.

QUESTIONS AND PROCEDURES

1. What is the overall quality of the financial statements? Are they complex and not readily understood? Are there any mysterious or unexplained line items on the balance sheet, income, or cash flow statements? Are the notes to the statements clear and understood?

2. What is the overall quality, competence, and depth of management? Identify officers, managers, or other key employees who will remain with the business, will depart, for whom tenure is unknown? List any key vacancies.

3. Are the cultures of the buyer and seller's organizations relatively similar, or are there substantial differences in management styles and treatment of customers and employees?

4. What has been the impact of globalization upon this business? Identify all present international cost, technological, and competitive pressures on the business. How has the business reacted to globalization? What trends in globalization are seen as positive or negative for the business?

5. Construct two preliminary financial five-year financial forecasts based on available information, one if the business remains under present ownership, and another if it is acquired.

6. Review any financial projections or recast earnings prepared by the seller and/or the seller's financial advisors or other representatives. Demand a complete list of all assumptions used in their preparation.

7. Does this business have any technological advantages or disadvantages? Are any emerging or known technologies a threat to the business?

8. Is the industry in which this business operates undergoing major changes that could have a negative impact?

9. Is there any indication of illegal activity, gross improprieties, deceitful accounting, or any dishonest management practices? Have any shareholders, directors, or officers ever been convicted or accused of a felony?

10. What has been the total compensation of the top three executives of the business for the past year? What commitments have been made for their future compensation? What benefits are they contractually entitled to in the event of their termination or a change in the control of the business?

11. Do any shareholders, officers, or directors have financial interests in other businesses or partnerships conducting business with this business?

12. Is this business involved with hedging or the use of any financial instruments that are considered derivatives? If yes, identify and quantify the potential downside risk. Are there risks that should be hedged?

13. Has the business been involved in incurring debt through the use of complex financial instruments or any other financial engineering techniques that would commonly be considered as unique, unorthodox, or unconventional?

14. Are there any off-balance sheet entities, and is their purpose both known and fully understood?

15. Does this business conduct business or sell services or products in industries, states, or countries where bribes or kickbacks are known or suspected to be common? If yes, what have been the practices of this business? Has this business been charged, or could it be charged, under the Foreign Corrupt Practices Act?

16. Identify and determine causes of any significant trends or changes in revenues, profits, or financial ratios. Are any inconsistent with those commonly found in the industry?

17. During the past five years, what new product lines, divisions, and acquisitions have been added to the business? What was the rational for each addition? What has been their revenue and operating profit each year? Are forecasts being achieved?

18. During the past five years, what product lines or business units have been sold, spun off, or liquidated? What revenues, operating profits, or losses did they account for in their last two years of operation? What was the rational for each deletion?

19. Are there any significant environmental issues that are known or suspected?

20. Is the business involved in or threatened with any significant litigation? Identify all litigation in progress and estimate, if possible, the probable outcome and date of final settlement.

21. Could the business be adversely affected by tariffs, regulatory changes, and/or enforcement?

22. What has been the cash flow for the past five years? Are there significant and unexplained differences between income statements, cash flow reports, and tax returns?

23. List all significant income for the current and past five years that could be considered extraordinary or nonrecurring. Separate the operating and nonoperating income. Review the accounting for any acquisitions made during this period.

24. List all significant expenses for the current and each of the past five years that could be considered as extraordinary or nonrecurring.

25. Are there any unusual and/or extraordinary expenses that are known to have a high probability of occurring in the next five years?

26. Is there any portion of the current income stream that for any reason may cease or be drastically reduced during the next five years? Are there any large contracts about to expire, be renegotiated, or terminated?

27. What were the capital expenditures for the past five years? What are planned for the current year? Compare actual expenditures to budgets and depreciation levels. What are planned and/or will be required during the next five years? Have necessary capital expenditures been delayed, and are there pressing requirements for capital expenditures?

28. Identify the activities of the business that are most profitable and their percentage of total operating income.

29. Identify the activities of the business that are least profitable.

30. Are there significant sources of nonoperating income, such as licensing fees, royalties, dividends, interest, and rental income? Determine how long each will continue.

31. Have earnings increased every quarter? Is there any indication that earnings have been manipulated to show steady growth?

32. Has this business made any acquisitions in which there are continuing obligations to the sellers?

33. Are any subsidiaries, divisions, or other major assets scheduled or being considered for divestment? Evaluate the circumstances, status, and wisdom of the decision to divest of any operations or assets now classified as discontinued.

34. Are any employees of such importance that their departure for any reason would jeopardize the existence of the business?

35. Do any shareholders or key executives have a propensity for litigation?

36. Why is this business for sale, or is there reason to believe it can be acquired? What is believed to be the motivation of selling investors?

37. Does the company have any anti-takeover defenses or barriers to a transaction, such as poison pills, loan covenants, buy-sell agreements, or generous change of control compensation agreements? If yes, obtain copies.

38. Have the major shareholders, directors, or officers engaged in serious discussions or negotiations within the past five years to sell the business? If yes, what were the full circumstances, including reason for failure? Has this deal been shopped? Are other potential buyers evaluating the deal, and at what stage are they in their evaluation?

39. Are there any emerging threats or negative factors not previously disclosed? Consider technological, competitive, and market changes that could affect the income of the business.

40. Review the representations and warranties the buyer will expect or demand from the seller. Are there any that will be difficult or impossible to obtain?

CHAPTER 4
Ownership and Capital Structure

PRIMARY ISSUES AND OBSERVATIONS

A. Two questions of critical importance must be quickly resolved: who owns the business, and what is the capital structure of the business? The answers may be clear and obvious, but frequently they are obscure and difficult to obtain. The answers to these questions, as much as possible, should have been acquired prior to this due diligence study, but all must be confirmed.

B. An understanding of the legal structure will aid in the identification of the owners and determining the extent of their ownership. If it is a corporation, there must be shareholders. If it is a partnership, there must be partners. Exactly who are the shareholders or partners and the amount of their ownership, along with their rights, becomes an important early issue. Complicating matters is that the percentage of ownership may not be fully indicative of the influence over the other shareholders or partners.

C. A difficult issue in any negotiations is the actual authority of the seller's negotiators to deliver whatever is negotiated. Early in discussions, the buyer should question the authority of whomever they are negotiating with to make commitments and complete the deal. Additional approvals required, such as from a board of directors, creditors, key shareholders, or partners, should be disclosed very early. Ownership issues must be resolved to determine if a transaction is possible. Who are the owners? Can they sell? Are some in favor of a sale and others opposed? Will they sell, and what obstacles exist that could prevent them from selling? All aspects of ownership and authority had best be sorted out before due diligence, but all should be verified in the due diligence process.

QUESTIONS AND PROCEDURES

1. What is the legal structure of the business under study? Is it a regular (C-Corp) corporation, S-corporation, partnership, limited partnership, sole proprietorship, subsidiary, division, product line, family limited partnership, or no structure, only designated assets and liabilities?

2. Obtain for review copies of incorporation, bylaws, partnership agreements, or other documents creating the business. Review minutes of board of directors meetings. If the business is a corporation, is it legally constituted and in good standing?

3. If a purchase of designated assets and liabilities are contemplated, obtain evidence of the owner's authority to consummate a transaction.

4. If the business is a corporation, determine the number of common shares issued, number of shares authorized, number of treasury shares, and if there is more than one class of common shares.

5. If the common stock is publicly traded, determine the recent price per share, date of price, four-year price range, book value, and average weekly and monthly volume of shares traded. Obtain published charts of stock activity.

6. Has the business issued any bonds, preferred shares, warrants, debentures, convertible securities, or any other type of security? If any have been issued, obtain documents creating the security, history including reasons for creating the security, amount outstanding, names of holders, and estimated value of the security. If any are publicly traded, ascertain the current market price and history of price and volume. If they are not publicly traded, have there been any recent private sales, and at what price?

7. If any of the securities of the business are rated by rating agencies, obtain the most recent ratings.

8. If the business is a private company, what ownership transfers of its securities have occurred during the past three years, and at what price? Who were the buyers and sellers and the reasons for the transfers? Are there buy-sell or other agreements limiting to whom shares can be sold?

9. Request a list of all shareholders, partners, limited partners, or other type of owner and the number of shares, securities, units, or other forms of ownership held.

    a) Will any be difficult to locate?

    b) Are any held in trusts or in estates?

10. What has been the company's dividend policy and payment history for all securities to shareholders or partners for the past five years? Are current practices expected to continue?

11. Has the company defaulted in the past or is in default on any debt or security covenants? If yes, what actions have the security holders taken or threatened? What is required to cure the default?

12. Do any debt agreements or securities contain provisions that could effect control of the business or restrict sale of shares?

13. Does the company have any stock or security buy-back obligations to the holders? Request a copy of the agreements. How will the buy-backs be financed?

14. Do any shareholders have obligations or preferential rights to purchase other shareholder's shares? Request copies of any buy-sell agreements.

15. Have any shares changed hands, and at what price under a buy-sell agreement?

16. Has the company had, or are there any, stock repurchase programs in progress? Have warrants or options been repurchased, or are there outstanding obligations to do so?

17. Determine the reasons for any changes in the number of shares authorized, issued, or in the treasury during the past three years.

18. If shares are public, on what stock exchanges do the companies securities trade? Who are the market makers? Request copies of any security analyst reports. Estimate the level of liquidity in the stock.

19. Are any securities registration statements in progress or being contemplated? If yes, what is the purpose and how would it effect this transaction?

20. Does the company have an ESOP plan? If yes:

    a) Request a copy of the plan.

    b) What is the plan's history, including why it was established?

    c) Who votes the plan's shares?

    d) Are the shares valued realistically?

    e) Request a copy of original and last valuation.

21. In general, are the share or security prices higher or lower in price or value than when the holders invested? If possible, determine the tax base for the major investors.

22. Does the business maintain a financial public relations program? Who meets and communicates with the security analysts?

23. Is there a formal or informal program of informing and nurturing shareholder relations? Are shareholders given discounts on the company's products or services?

24. Is there a stock purchase program for employees? If yes, obtain full details. What percentage of outstanding shares is owned by employees?

25. Is there a dividend reinvestment program for shareholders?

26. What major partners, shareholders, officers, or directors have bought or sold shares in the past two years? List all trades during the past two years reported as "inside trades."

27. Have any securities, options, or warrants that were not part of a formal program been given or repurchased? If yes, what were the circumstances and price?

28. Obtain copies of any outstanding stock option plans and a list of all participants, the number of options held, and date they may be exercised. Do all the options become vested if ownership of the business changes?

    a) How are decisions made to select participants and number of shares?

    b) Obtain a list of options exercised in the past two years.

    c) How are options recorded on the financial statements?

    d) Is there any evidence of "back dating" options?

    e) Is there any evidence of "spring loading" prior to favorable news?

    f) Are optioned shares repurchased by the company or sold on the open market?

    g) What programs, if any, does the company have to assist in the purchase or tax consequences of optioned shares?

29. Who are the major shareholders or partners, and what is their role in managing the business? What was their initial investment, and what would be the amount they would realize if the business was sold? Compare their present income from the business with the income they would have if the business was sold.

30. What are the reputations of the controlling shareholders or partners?

CHAPTER 5
Directors and Governance

PRIMARY ISSUES AND OBSERVATIONS

A. Many business organizations are structured without a board of directors or some sort of governing body. Sole proprietorships are usually controlled by one individual, and partnerships by the partners or a limited partner. In closely held private corporations, a board may exist primarily to meet legal requirements and often consists largely of family members. However, most businesses are formed as corporations with boards of directors, and their role and level of activity requires study. If there is no board, this chapter is irrelevant.

B. While a director's legal responsibilities are fairly clear, their actual role in making major decisions and in governing the business is extremely variable. From an investor's perspective, the director's role is of importance in that the directors must approve or at least acquiesce to any proposed major transaction. Should the transaction involve acquisition of the entire corporation, the directors will normally submit resignations to become effective at time of closing. Divestitures of significant businesses or assets will require board approval in most corporations. As a result of the board's final decision-making authority, an investor needs insight into how the board functions and the personal effects the transaction may have upon individual directors. A critical question during any negotiation is the authority and support their negotiators have from the board.

C. The financial impact upon the business of the elimination of the directors should be positive, but this is not certain and requires study. Elimination of their compensation is an obvious benefit, but some directors may have played a key role in establishing and maintaining business relationships beneficial to the business. The probability of continuing the relationships in the absence of the director requires evaluation and, if necessary, steps taken to preserve the relationships. Of course, some relationships may have benefited a director more than the business, and this is an opportunity to end the relationship.

QUESTIONS AND PROCEDURES

1. Obtain a list of company directors. Determine their background, business affiliations, other board memberships, and length of time on the board. Identify the directors who are most influential in setting policy and deciding significant issues.

2. What were the reasons or circumstances that resulted in the election of each member of the board? What are believed to be the contributions of each board member to the success or failure of the business?

3. What compensation do the directors receive? Include fees per meeting, salaries, options, pension benefits, termination pay, perquisites, and any other items of value.

4. How many shares and/or options does each director own?

5. Calculate the financial benefit for each director if the business is sold or merged. Include sale of shares, options exercised, separation pay, pensions, broker or finder fees, or any other financial benefits.

6. What are the terms of office for the directors? Are terms staggered?

7. Are any board members affiliated with, or have a financial interest in, any businesses or financial institutions that conduct business with the business under study? If yes, obtain complete details.

8. Are there any business relationships that would be in jeopardy or cease if any director was terminated? If yes, obtain details and determine if the business would be helped or damaged.

9. Have any board members resigned or not stood for reelection in the past three years?

10. How often does the board meet? Where? Are board meetings a combination of business, social, or vacation activities?

11. What is the board's actual role in setting policy and overseeing the business? Does the board only ratify what the CEO proposes? Is there any evidence that the board has disagreed with and overruled management decisions or recommendations?

12. Determine and evaluate the relationship between the board and the CEO. Is the CEO dominant? Is the relationship one of cooperation, acquiescence, dissatisfaction, or hostility?

13. Determine the names of the committees of the board and the members of each committee. Obtain any committee reports issued in the last five years.

14. How vigorously do the committees pursue their responsibilities? Are they active and aggressive or only a rubber stamp for management?

15. Describe in detail how the compensation committee reaches decisions. If compensation consultants are retained, obtain their name, amounts paid, copies of their reports, and recommendations. Do any of these consultants perform other services for the business? Are there possible conflicts of interest?

16. Describe in detail the activities of the audit committee.

17. Is there any evidence of splits or factions within the board? If splits exist, are they affecting the operations of the business?

18. How are the directors protected from liability? Review a copy of the policy providing insurance coverage for director liability.

19. If the business has subsidiaries, what is the role of subsidiary directors in overseeing the subsidiaries?

20. Does the company have directors appointed to joint ventures or companies in which less than 100 percent of the shares are owned? If yes, obtain full details.

21. If there are companies, joint ventures, or partnerships less than 100 percent owned by the company, request full information on the other shareholders or partners, including their rights, estimated value of their investment, general reputation, and status of relations with them.

22. Are there any active and vocal critics of the board, directors, management, or controlling owners? If yes, obtain full details, including the issues involved.

23. Describe a typical or, if possible, the last two shareholder meetings? What was the attendance, atmosphere, events, etc.? What is the format of the meetings? Are nondirectors asked to attend and participate or make presentations? Does an attorney attend regularly? If yes, identify the attorney.

24. Have there been any cancelled, special, or delayed meetings?

25. Obtain and review the minutes of the board of directors meetings.

26. Does the board or any of its members have a strong interest in and advocate policies on social issues and climate change?

CHAPTER 6
Management

PRIMARY ISSUES AND OBSERVATIONS

A. The composition and quality of the seller's management should be under continuous study and evaluation during the due diligence investigation. A buyer usually presents himself as one who will retain all the "good" people, and seller personnel are in the position of having to indicate they will accept a new owner. Often the behavior on both sides tends to be less than truthful, with the buyer not certain of his personnel plans until the evaluation is complete, and the seller personnel skeptical of any buyer assurances. Seller personnel are in a particularly difficult position if they possess negative company information that could jeopardize the deal, but if not revealed may damage their careers with a new owner.

Management built the organization, runs it today, and will be required in the future. The questions in this chapter can be answered with specific facts, but the larger issues of the competence of individuals and the management team as a whole are subjective evaluations requiring judgment and care. The seller management is responsible for a business attractive enough for the investor to pursue, so it would be inappropriate to draw either positive or negative hasty opinions regarding individuals or the entire team. Evaluation of management is difficult, requiring perceptive personnel involved in the evaluation process. Direct interviews are essential, and reliance only on the opinions of management peers or employees is a mistake. Interviews are also an opportunity to extol the investors and allay fears and misconceptions of seller personnel.

B. The four "Cs" of management due diligence are: competence, compatibility, continuity, and compensation. An in-depth understanding of all four should be the primary objective. Competence is simply how well individuals are performing their jobs. The question of compatibility with the buyer's style of management and culture should not be glossed over but given careful study. There are many ways to run successful businesses, and no one way is best. However, it is certain that within an organization, only one way is possible at any given time. Recognizing that there are always some differences between organizations, the fundamental question becomes: can the differences between the investor and seller organizations be resolved or overcome without adversely affecting the businesses? Management and cultural clashes are contributing, if not primary, causes in most acquisitions that failed to meet the buyer's expectations. Continuity involves the issues of how many managers will remain and the damage done by those who may terminate. Compensation is the problem of how the compensation levels of the buyer and seller's management compare.

C. Management is usually viewed as a team, but the chief executive officers (CEOs), past and present, have established and implemented the policies of the business that have made it whatever it is today. Start with a study of the role of the CEO and the impact the incumbent has had upon the business, keeping in mind that this individual in most cases will have great influence, if not determine, how the negotiations will be concluded. An evaluation of the CEO's past and current accomplishments, strategy, and management style will facilitate an understanding of his importance to the business, the desirability of continued tenure, and, if necessary, the characteristics to be sought in a replacement. The study should continue to evaluate other members of the team considered management, and while the entire team is being evaluated, necessary emphasis will be on individuals.

Identification of key management members is a critical first step, but not always a simple one. Officers may not always be key employees, and key employees may not always be officers. Job titles and job descriptions can be misleading. Compensation may not always indicate importance to the future of the business, since share holdings, age, former positions, and relationships can all influence current compensation.

QUESTIONS AND PROCEDURES

1. How long has the CEO been in his present position, and how and why was he selected?

2. Describe the policies and strategies of the CEO that have been successful, unsuccessful, and those too early to evaluate. To what degree have the CEO's policies had an impact upon the business? Does the CEO have a strategic plan communicated to all managers and employees?

3. How would one characterize the CEO's style of management? Hands-on, micromanages, delegates broad responsibility, inspirational, determined, ruthless, etc.? Has the CEO imposed a business style and culture upon the organization? Describe the techniques the CEO uses to communicate his instructions.

4. How is the CEO viewed by other managers, employees, customers, and the community?

5. Is there any evidence of friction between the CEO and any directors or major shareholders?

6. What is the power structure, both formal and informal, to make major decisions?

7. Request a list of all officers and key employees, their titles, age, length of service, brief job description, and summary of their background.

8. Obtain or create an organization chart illustrating the reporting relationships of all officers and key employees.

9. List all officers and key employees who have signed employment contracts and/or confidentiality agreements. Obtain copies.

10. Have any officers or employees refused to sign employment contracts and/or confidentiality agreements?

11. Request complete compensation information on all officers and key employees for the past three years, including the current year. Include all types of compensation: salary, bonuses, options and other types of stock rewards, retirement benefits, golden parachutes, loans, and perquisites. Obtain copies of their contracts.

12. Obtain copies of any management incentive plans based on performance. What are the criteria for measuring performance? What amounts have been paid to each executive under the plans, and what are their potential earnings under the plan? What is the duration of the plan?

13. Describe the effect a change of control could trigger, including, but not limited to, the following: early vesting of options, accelerated performance incentives, restricted shares, performance shares, termination pay, etc.

14. What are the "tax gross up" obligations? What commitments have been made to cover the cost of executive taxes on compensation and benefits payable upon termination? Estimate the potential cost.

15. Determine the total cost for each of the business's four top executives. Include direct compensation, options, fringe benefits, perquisites, travel and entertainment expenses, and secretarial or other employee assistants.

16. Rank the officers and executives in order of actual authority or power within the business. To whom do employees look to make or influence major decisions?

17. If any officers or key employees have been in their present positions for less than two years, determine the factors influencing their selection and the reason for their selection.

18. Are there presently any unfilled executive or key employee vacancies?

19. Are there any officers or key employees likely to change positions within the business, quit, retire, or be terminated for any reason? Identify any officers or key employees with serious health problems.

20. Are there logical successors for the most important executives? Is there a program to identify and develop highly qualified managers for promotion?

21. What is the CEO's opinion of the overall strength and depth of management? Are his opinions shared by others in the organization?

22. Is there nepotism in the business? Does the business have a formal policy on nepotism? List all relatives of shareholders, directors, officers, and managers employed in the business and their positions and compensation. Are any overcompensated and/or work less than full time? Are there any romantic "affairs" within management that are detrimental to the business or would be embarrassing to the company if exposed?

23. Are there officers or key employees who could severely damage the business if they left the business on a hostile basis?

24. Are there any key employees so important to the business that they are nearly irreplaceable and the business would be severely damaged if they departed for any reason?

25. Are there any officers or key employees who do not work full time for the business? If yes, obtain a full explanation.

26. Are there any shareholders, officers, employees, consultants, friends, or relatives who are paid for little or no work? If yes, obtain full information.

27. Do any officers or key employees have health problems that impair their performance? Are any suspected of alcoholism or drug addiction?

28. Do any officers or key employees have hobbies, investments, business activities, charitable activities, or any other interests that prevent them from devoting full time to their positions?

29. Is there any evidence of past or present officers, managers, or employees having conflicts of interest? Search for conflicts, such as owning an interest in a business that conducts business with this one, leasing property to the business, participating in a partnership of which the business is a partner, etc.

30. Identify perquisites, other than normal fringe benefits enjoyed by officers and key employees. List and determine the cost of executive dining

rooms, apartments, aircraft, country clubs, and hunting, fishing, ski, or other lodges owned or frequented at company expense. Are these facilities used by only the CEO or a small number of senior executives?

31. List any business owned or leased recreational facilities, boats, and aircraft. What percentage of the use may be considered as personal? Identify facilities used exclusively by senior management.

32. Are any employees who are shareholders paid bonuses in lieu of dividends?

33. Do any officers, directors, or key employees have national or international recognition or prominence for any reason in any field.

34. What is the general reputation of management? How is management viewed by customers, employees, the community, shareholders, and the general public?

35. Have any major shareholders, officers, directors, or key employees been associated with any businesses that failed, accused of criminal conduct, or been involved in any situation considered scandalous or improper?

36. Has the business's organization been relatively stable, or have reorganizations occurred within the past three years? Is any internal reorganization in progress or planned? If yes to either, what was or is the purpose?

37. Have management consultants been retained within the past three years? If yes, what were their assignments, cost, and results?

38. Has this management utilized management techniques advocated by consultants that are of controversial value or considered fads by others? Does management pride itself on introducing managerial innovations?

39. How would you characterize management's style and the overall culture of the organization and how compatible is it with a buyer's? What, if any, are the major differences?

40. Review the overall depth of management. Is this an asset, or a serious shortcoming? Are there logical successors for most key executives, or will recruiting from the outside be necessary?

CHAPTER 7

Products and Services

PRIMARY ISSUES AND OBSERVATIONS

A. Revenues and operating income from products, commodities, and services sold by the business are its lifeblood. Financial statements should be viewed as only a portion of the picture in efforts to fully understand a business and its potential. Extraordinary income by definition does not reoccur, and nonoperating income may be transitory. Financial reports record history, but actual present sales, backlogs of unfilled orders, estimates of growth, or declines of products and services are the best indications of the future. Pro-forma forecasts of future revenues and profits have limited value in the absence of an understanding of the underlying product and service lines. Reliable forecasts and budgets are built from the bottom up, rather than the top down.

B. Comprehensive due diligence requires gauging the importance of individual products and services to the business. Public perceptions and initial impressions often deviate from reality because many businesses are best known for activity representing only a small fraction of their total business. Investors often are attracted by a product or service line but learn it is small and accompanied by the baggage of the rest of the business. A business may have a famous name, but the products or services that brought the name to prominence may have declined or been replaced. Actual amounts and proportions of revenues and operating profits for individual lines may prove to be a surprise.

C. The business's organizational structure and accounting system may for evaluation purposes reflect what constitutes a product or service. The more detailed the accounting breakdown, the more valuable the information will be to the investor. The existing accounting system that tends to track the organization structure will largely determine the amount of information available. However, there may be supplemental records and reports prepared by product line managers for their own use that are not a part of the formal accounting system and should be requested. Accounting systems vary widely in reporting profitability of product lines, and the results can become very subjective when overhead allocations are made. The result can be highly profitable or unprofitable product line segments concealed in broad financial reports. The required breakdown of product revenues and gross profits appearing in annual reports give a broad view, but the categories are often so broad that they are only a starting point in due diligence investigation.

QUESTIONS AND PROCEDURES

1. Define precisely the products and services sold by the business. Review the organization and accounting system to learn how the business recognizes and defines each product or service offered. ("Services" is a broad category that includes most sources of operating income other than the sale of manufactured products and commodities.)

2. List all products and services sold by the business and the total revenues, including gross and pretax profits each represents. Obtain data for the last three years and year-to-date data.

3. For each product, commodity, or service line, obtain a breakdown of the cost of sales into material, labor, and overhead. Considering the resultant gross profit, how significant is each of these categories?

4. Identify products or services experiencing declines in gross margin, and learn of the causes.

5. Obtain copies of all product literature and catalogs.

6. Obtain and review copies of trade publications covering activities of the industries in which each product or service line functions.

7. Request copies of any studies conducted either internally or by consultants on the subject of product or service line profitability, life expectancy, or market position.

8. Estimate the remaining market life and growth potential of the major products and services. Prepare five-year forecasts. In cases of major contracts for products or projects, when will the contracts be complete, and what is the probability of similar contracts?

9. Are there any products or services that presently have relatively small sales but management believes have great potential for growth?

10. Are any products or services threatened with technological obsolescence?

11. Are there products or services with which the business enjoys a technological advantage over competitors? If yes, how long will the advantage survive?

12. Are any products or services considered fads, subject to fashion changes, or changes in customer tastes?

13. Are any products or services, either by design or through market conditions, expected to have a limited life?

14. Does the business have any products or services that are under consideration or scheduled to be discontinued or phased out?

15. For each line, what percentages of annual revenues and profits are for after-sale service, maintenance, or enhancements?

16. For each line, what percentages of annual revenues and profits are for repair or replacement parts? What is the gross profits percentage on parts sold?

17. For each line, what percentages of revenues and profits are for expendables?

18. Are there competitors supplying parts or expendables? If yes, is this a serious problem, and how is it combated?

19. Compare the gross profit margins on spare parts and/or expendables with the original equipment.

20. Does the business have any contracts with customers that may be difficult to fill for any reason, such as pricing, available raw material, labor difficulties, delivery schedule, or meeting specifications? If yes, obtain full information and the extent of possible losses, if any.

21. What products or services are scheduled to be introduced in the next two years? Are any behind schedule? What is the cost of development, capital equipment, and introduction of each? What revenues and profits are forecast for each? Obtain copies of any internal studies or reports relative to these new products or services.

22. What performance or quality guarantees are normally given? Request copies of the written guarantees and warranties. Are any informal guarantees given or implied?

23. How is product service provided, managed, and charged? Identify any third parties authorized to provide service.

24. Has any product been recalled or under consideration to be recalled? Have any alleged defects resulted in personal injuries?

25. What warranties and guarantees are given? Are there any outstanding that deviate from written practices? Obtain copies of all warranties and guarantees.

26. Have warranty costs, claims, and exposure been a significant factor in this business's operations?

    a) Request a list of major causes of warranty claims.

    b) What was last year's warranty expense and the estimated future exposure?

    c) What is the amount reserved for warranty claims and is it adequate?

    d) Are there any trends indicating warranty claims are increasing or decreasing?

    e) Have warranty claims, either questionable or fictional, ever been used to conceal improper or illegal payments?

27. Are there substantial seasonal variations in the level of business for any of the lines? If yes, determine how it affects all aspects of the business, production, inventory levels, inventory, cash flow, and profits.

28. If this business provides services on an hourly basis, what are the hourly billing charges, and how are the hours controlled? Have customers complained of excessive hours billed?

29. If this business is in a rental or leasing business, are sales of assets and "involuntary conversions" an important source of income? Who handles such sales?

30. Is there a problem with counterfeit or "knock-off" products? If yes, describe the extent of the problem and steps being taken for control.

31. Identify products or services sold to government agencies. Is any of this work of a classified nature? If yes, what level of secrecy is required?

32. If the business is engaged in the production and/or marketing of commodities, such as petroleum products, gas, grains, and metals, does it enter into forward contracts requiring delivery at a fixed price? If yes, what has been its experience? Obtain a list of all outstanding forward contracts. Who is responsible for negotiating forward contracts?

CHAPTER 8
R&D and Technology

PRIMARY ISSUES AND OBSERVATIONS

A. A comprehensive study of research and development often requires a team effort. An investigator with financial background can review the financial records, budgets, and projections. A scientist, consultant, and/or engineer may be necessary to evaluate research in progress or contemplated. Marketing people may estimate the market size and potential for the research if successful. A patent attorney may be necessary to study the validity of any patents and voice an opinion on existing or threatened disputes. The broad effort is necessary, since the future of the business may depend upon R&D success. An objective evaluation is often difficult because of its importance to an individual's career and his honest, but not always realistic, optimism for his projects.

B. All R&D is both a current expense and an investment in the future of the business. What the eventual return on the investment will be is never known in advance with certainty because of the many variables, not all of which are controlled by the business. There has to exist a level of faith in the technical people, and that will largely be based on past performance and their ability to present convincing arguments. The level of present funding for R&D represents management's judgment considering all factors, including available financial resources. Other potential results—with a different level of funding or redirected emphasis in the R&D program—should be a major area of study for any investor.

C. Prior to commencing the study, define the terms research, development, and technology as used in both the investor's and seller's businesses. What in one business may be considered research, in another may be development or the exact opposite. Technology for some may be a very narrow term referring only to developments resulting from research, while for others a very broad definition may be used to include know-how, trade secrets, and marketing information. Unless the definitions are first determined, answers to the questions may be misleading.

QUESTIONS AND PROCEDURES

1. Is this business engaged in research and development? If yes, how is R&D organized and structured within the business? Is one person in charge of R&D, or is responsibility dispersed? Identify the person in charge and/or other key personnel and their backgrounds. Identify any attorneys involved in patent and intellectual property issues.

2. Define research. How is the expense recorded in the financial statements?

3. Define development. How is the expense recorded in the financial statements?

4. Define technology as used by this business. Is its reputation for technology a fair description, exaggerated, or understated? Does it have a record and reputation for innovation?

5. If possible, segregate expenses for research and development into categories in which the objectives are either new products, methods, or processes to be utilized in creating or manufacturing new products or services.

6. Describe the business's R&D programs, including past history, objectives, expenditures, manpower, and results.

7. Identify all R&D contracted out. Obtain the names of the contractors, amount spent and/or committed to each. What have been the results, and what results are anticipated?

8. Does the business have a close working relationship with any universities? If yes, identify the universities and describe the relationship and advantages to both.

9. What R&D is this business performing for others? If yes, how is this work billed? Identify any R&D work performed for a government.

10. Are R&D expenses in total increasing or decreasing?

11. Review the level of coordination between R&D, marketing, and manufacturing required for commercialization of new products. Is this a problem area?

12. List new products or services introduced as a result of the R&D programs in the past five years? Identify those that have had a significant financial

impact upon the business, including any "home runs." Identify those that have been a disappointment or failure.

13. Obtain copies of internal R&D budgets, plans, and objectives.

14. What products, processes, or services are under development, and when are they expected to be commercially available or placed into use? Will any replace existing products, processes, or services?

15. Have any new products been announced but are not fully developed?

16. Are time tables being met? Are any significantly behind schedule? Have timetables been met during the past three years?

17. How many graduate engineers, scientists, or other professionals are engaged in R&D work? How many have PhDs? Are employees encouraged to attend professional meetings and write peer-reviewed papers?

18. List any technology or know-how, not patented or licensed, that is critical to the operation of the business or gives a competitive advantage.

19. For each of the past two fiscal years and the current year to date, what was the royalty or license income received? What is forecast for the next five years? Obtain copies of the license agreements. Who is responsible for monitoring the collections?

20. During the current fiscal year, what is the amount estimated to be paid to others for royalties or license fees? How long will these obligations continue? Are fees being paid for technology no longer in use? Obtain copies of the licenses and/or royalty agreements.

21. Are there any licensing agreements critical to the business's financial success either as a licensee or licensor? When do they terminate? Identify any cross-licensing agreements.

22. Are there any disputes, existing or threatened, with licensees or licensors?

23. List all valid patents owned or licensed by the business and their date of expiration. Describe their purpose and application and importance to the business. Are any being challenged? Obtain copies of those of importance.

24. Do any businesses, individuals, employees, or former employees have any rights or royalty income from patents owned by the business?

25. Does the business have disputes of any kind with inventors or those claiming to be inventors?

26. What are the products being developed subject to government approval or independent laboratories? If yes, describe the agencies, approval process, and any problems inherent to the system.

27. What security procedures does the company have to protect its technology? Is this a major concern? Is there a formal policy?

28. List any R&D funded by the government. What is the magnitude of the funding, the probability of continuance, and the prospects for future funding? What rights does the business retain to use the results of the R&D?

29. Are the patents owned by the business assigned to an independent or affiliated company primarily for tax advantages? If yes, obtain complete information.

30. Does there exist within the business any controversy over the viability or safety of either products under development or on the market?

31. Is this business in an industry where theft of R&D and trade secrets has occurred?

32. Has the business been accused of stealing trade secrets or R&D, or has it accused others? If yes, what was the outcome?

CHAPTER 9
Markets and Customers

PRIMARY ISSUES AND OBSERVATIONS

A. Markets change and customers come and go. Any study should assume present conditions are a base point of great importance, but they are by no means a certain indication of future market conditions. Trends in today's markets may prove to be the best indication of the future. There is a large amount of information from public and private sources that should be sought and analyzed to arrive at reasonable conclusions.

B. Precisely who the customers are and the probability of their continuing on may be difficult to ascertain. If possible, interviews with customers are desirable. For some businesses, only categories of customers can be studied because there are no significant individual customers as in retailing, lodging, and transportation. Often representative samples can be helpful. In other businesses, important customers may only buy once or infrequently, such as in the construction and capital equipment industries. If the business is not a cash business, a review of receivables can be the best source to identify present customers.

C. There are many sources of information to learn the size of markets and changes underway.

a) Obtain or subscribe to industry trade publications and request back issues.

b) Obtain industry studies prepared by security analysts.

c) Review seller's receivables to learn names of active customers.

d) Search the Internet for information.

e) Contact any trade associations to which the seller belongs or could be a member. Seek data on market share.

f) Contact the business's advertising agency for data they may have.

QUESTIONS AND PROCEDURES

1. Identify the business's executives who have the best knowledge of the markets and customers. Obtain their opinions and answers to the questions. Request copies of any marketing and/or industry studies they may possess.

2. Describe the markets into which the seller's products and/or services are sold. What defines the markets, geography, price, quality, etc.?

3. Describe the customers served in each market.

4. Estimate the size of each market, both domestically and internationally. Indicate sources of estimates.

5. Are the markets growing or declining? Are there discernable trends?

6. What is the market share for each product or service of the business? Are the percentages increasing, decreasing, or stable?

7. Identify new markets the business has entered in the past two years. Does management have plans to enter new markets? If yes, identify the markets and stage of entering.

8. Identify any demographic trends affecting this business either positively or negatively.

9. What are the business's main geographical markets? Are there plans to expand into new markets?

10. Has the business withdrawn from any markets within the past four years? If yes, determine causes?

11. What is the general state of the industries in which the business's products or services compete? What are the significant trends, if any, in marketing approach, pricing, new products or services, manufacturing, government regulations, global expansion, etc.? Are these industries growing or declining?

12. Are there acquisitions creating consolidations within the industries in which the business operates? If yes, what is the impact upon this business?

13. If applicable, for each product or service line, list the 10 largest customers and the percentage of total sales each represents. If possible, compare this list with the customers from two years previous.

14. Are any major customers in danger of being lost to competitors, financial difficulties, or other known causes?

15. Are there any disputes with any customers? Who handles customer complaints?

16. Identify significant customers added within the past three years.

17. Identify major customers lost within the past three years and the circumstances.

18. Has the business been terminated from any jobs or orders cancelled prior to completion within the past three years? If yes, obtain complete details.

19. How do customers view this business? How would they react to the business being acquired?

20. At what level of a customer's organization is the buying decision made? How many must be "sold" to affect a sale?

21. Are the markets seasonal? If yes, how does it affect the operations of the business?

22. Have there been any studies or estimates of customer turnover? How many are new, and how many disappear each year?

23. For each product or service line, estimate the percentage of revenues from repeat customers.

24. Is this business selling in any areas considered hazardous or markets in which bribes and kickbacks are common?

CHAPTER 10
Competition

PRIMARY ISSUES AND OBSERVATIONS

A. Competition exists in several forms: direct, alternative products or services, and refusal to buy anything. Direct competition is the most prevalent, in the form of others providing similar products or services of comparable quality and price. Alternative products or services have similar functions but thrive because of price, quality, or service differences. Examples are the proliferation of counterfeit replacement parts and expendables and the proliferation of "knock-offs" in the fashion industry.

B. Competing executives often have unrealistic and inaccurate views of their competitors. Selling difficulties or failures may be blamed on alleged "unethical" competitive behavior. Rumors of problems competitors may or may not be experiencing tend to be repeated as fact. Most executives extol the virtues of a competitive market, but at the same time wish nothing but misfortune upon their competitors. Competitors may be more successful than their competitors believe, but they do exist, and most survive. It often is a challenge to obtain accurate and balanced information from executives of the business under study.

C. During the study of competitors, investors should be alert to any evidence or suspicion of noncompetitive or collusive activity with competitors. Since price fixing, dividing of markets, and bid collusion and the establishment of "orderly markets" is known to frequently exist, it is reasonable to start with the assumption that the practices may have occurred in the past and possibly still exist. The pressure to obtain profitable business makes it difficult to resist the temptation. Executives who have participated in such improprieties are unlikely to volunteer information since they are aware of the criminal consequences. The existence of illegal market activity may prove to be a "deal killer."

QUESTIONS AND PROCEDURES

1. Identify the major competing businesses for each product or service line. Separate domestic and international. Obtain Dun & Bradstreet financial reports and review Web pages of competitors. If there are no major competitors but many small businesses or individuals, describe their nature and estimate their share of the market.

2. Compare each competitor with the business studied. What is their market share? What advantages does each competitor enjoy, and what are the competitive advantages of the business understudy? Cover such items as cost, design, methods of marketing, pricing, discounts, service, quality, delivery, etc. Overall, which competitors are most effective and why?

3. Are any competitors engaged in expansion programs? Are any adding sales personnel, distribution centers, advertising, or Internet sales? Have any revised their strategy and become much more effective in the past two years?

4. What is management's opinion of its marketing and distribution methods and cost compared to competitors? Are changes in progress to better compete?

5. What do competitors think of this business?

6. Have any competitors been formed or are now managed by former employees?

7. Is the business obligated by, or does it hold, any noncompetition agreements or judgments restricting sales?

8. How will competitors react to this contemplated transaction? Will they be elated, dismayed, or indifferent?

9. Does the business belong to trade associations in which there are periodic meetings with competitors? Has there been a history or suspicion of meetings at which illegal practices were discussed? Are there informal meetings with competitors at trade association events?

10. Is there any evidence of price fixing, market sharing, or other improper collusion with competitors having occurred in the past or continuing to this day?

11. Has the business ever been charged with engaging in illegal marketing activity?

12. Are there any competitors that are now relatively small that appear to be a significant competitor in the future?

13. Are any competitors locked in with customers, making it impossible to sell to those customers? Do any competitors receive a "last look"?

14. Are any competitors suspected of paying bribes or kickbacks? If yes, does this represent a significant loss of business to the business under study?

15. Do any competitors offer customers expensive trips and entertainment or have recreational facilities such as hunting and fishing camps?

16. Are counterfeit parts, products, and "knock-offs" a problem? If yes, describe any countermeasures taken.

CHAPTER 11
Marketing, Selling, and Distribution

PRIMARY ISSUES AND OBSERVATIONS

A. The marketing organization, trade names, and established customer relations may be the most valuable assets of the business that are not reflected on the balance sheet. Since these assets are largely intangible, emphasis during the investigation should be on both learning its composition and estimating how well it can be retained.

B. The cost of marketing is all expense, and a constant challenge for every management is to determine the optimum level of expenditures. Are present expenses being well spent? Are selling expenses too high for the sales volume generated? Would larger expenditures produce greater profitable revenues and bottom line profits? The investor's investigators should gather enough information about current marketing expense to allow educated opinions on these questions.

C. As a consequence of the incentive and constant pressure to increase profits, management attention often becomes focused on the marketing program. In an effort to improve sales and contain costs, marketing organizations may have recently undergone changes, or changes are under study. Managements are seldom totally satisfied. The success or failure of major changes in marketing strategy during the past year should be evaluated along with any contemplated revisions.

QUESTIONS AND PROCEDURES

1. Describe the marketing organization. Request or sketch an organization chart. Identify all personnel, including inside support personnel. Request key personnel resumes and compensation data.

2. Describe the methods of selling and distribution for each product and/or service line, such as direct sales, distributors, retail, Internet, independent representatives, catalogs, telemarketing, etc.

3. Estimate the percentage of gross sales sold by each method.

4. Review contracts and compensation agreements with nonemployees, such as independent representatives and distributors. Are all the contracts current? For each, review their record of sales for the past two years. Identify those carrying an inventory of the business's products and the amount.

5. Describe changes in the marketing organization that have occurred in the past two years. What has been the result?

6. Describe changes made in marketing strategy during the past two years. What has been the result?

7. Describe changes in progress or planned in marketing methods, strategy, or for the marketing organization. Are alternate methods of marketing under serious consideration?

8. List the countries in which the business regularly obtains business and the dollar volume for each.

9. Request a list of foreign representatives and/or sales outlets and annual volume for each during the past two years.

10. What percentage of gross sales is sold domestically but exported?

11. What was the dollar volume of sales to any government or government agency during the past two years and expected during the current year? How are these products or services marketed, and to what agencies or departments?

12. Are any government contracts subject to renegotiation or cancellation?

13. Does this business have an overall marketing plan and strategy? If yes, request a copy. How does this plan differ from competitors?

14. Define selling expense, and determine the selling expense as a percentage of gross sales for each product or service line.

15. Determine the role, strategy, and importance of the following in the marketing program. Why do customers buy the products or services?
    - Price
    - Delivery
    - Quality

- Credit
- Post-purchase service and technical support
- Installation service
- Made-to-order products
- Competence of personnel
- Location
- Transportation expense
- Advertising and product literature
- Internet convenience
- Technology level
- Rebates
- Return policy
- Compensation for reps and distributors
- Tariffs
- Distributor, retailer, or dealer financing
- Customer financing
- Diversity of products or services
- Completeness of product line
- Personal relationships

16. Describe the inventory levels believed necessary to accommodate customers. Identify the inventory locations and the amount at each location.

17. If credit approval is a significant factor in the business, describe the credit approval system and organization. How important is it to the business?

18. Obtain a list of all brand names and estimate their value to the business. Are they copyrighted, and the copyrights defended? Are any under attack?

19. Are "just in time" deliveries necessary to accommodate customers production?

20. Compare the typical sales person's (reps or distributor personnel, if applicable) education and experience with what management considers ideal.

21. How difficult is it to employ new sales personnel? How many openings exist today?

22. Are salesmen recruited primarily because they have a following of customers?

23. Is there a sales training program? If yes, describe. What is the length of time in training and on the job required before a salesman is considered "fully qualified"?

24. Request a list of sales personnel currently employed, their sales volume, and compensation. Request a copy of their compensation plan.

25. Does the business provide or arrange financing for customers? If yes, describe in detail and obtain copies of all finance contracts. Is this financing with or without recourse? If yes, what is the exposure to the business? What is the source of the financing?

26. Does the business lease its products? If yes, what are the terms and obtain copies of all contracts. What is the source of financing? Does the business have financial exposure as a result of leasing?

27. Does the business provide financing or financial guarantees to distributors, agents, retailers, or dealers? What is the record of such transactions, and what is the probability of recovering funds advanced and maximum financial exposure?

28. What rights do distributors, dealers, and retailers have to return unsold merchandise? Are there restocking charges? Are returns a common occurrence?

29. Is this a business in which departing executives or sales personnel have, or are likely to take, their customers with them? Has this happened? What defenses does the business have?

30. Is there an active market for used equipment sold by the business? If yes, how does the business participate, and how is it affected?

31. Does this business conduct business in countries where bribes and unusual commissions are commonplace? If yes, how does this business conduct its business?

32. Has this business ever been charged or suspected of paying bribes and/ or kickbacks?

33. What emoluments are given as inducements to customers, such as costly gifts or entertainment, hunting and fishing trips, sporting events and theater, Christmas gifts, loans, kickbacks, etc.?

34. Is any portion of the business dependent upon government subsidies or grants, either directly or indirectly?

35. If the business is a franchisor, what is the total number of franchisees, annual turnover of franchise ownerships, and failure rate of franchisees? Identify areas of controversy, including litigation with franchisees.

36. Has this business been in compliance with all Department of Commerce regulations affecting exports? Who monitors compliance, and seeks approvals when necessary?

37. Is the reputation of this business and its executives an advantage, detriment, or immaterial to the marketing effort?

CHAPTER 12
Pricing

PRIMARY ISSUES AND OBJECTIVES

A. The pricing of products and services directly determines the profitability of the business, but it is often an area given inadequate attention by senior management and those conducting due diligence investigations. Is pricing given full management attention? Are there formalized or informal pricing policies? And how are pricing decisions made? Those are all questions requiring study.

B. Understanding pricing may be complex because the actual price realized for a product or service results after terms are factored in. Price lists are often little more than a starting point or a wish list. Discounts, payment terms, and price incentives all influence the final price received.

C. The basic question for any investigator is: Are prices at a level that can be increased or should be decreased?

QUESTIONS AND PROCEDURES

1. What is this business's philosophy or approach to pricing? Is management aggressive and innovative in pricing? Does it only match competitors or charge "what the market will bear"?

2. Does the business have written pricing policies? If yes, obtain copies. Are the policies well known and followed? Are there policies generally understood and followed, but not written?

3. How are prices and terms actually determined? Identify those who are involved. If prices are negotiated, who participates in the negotiations and what guidelines do they have?

4. Describe the influence each of the following has on prices:

- Cost to produce or provide service
- Competition
- Cost of transportation
- Production capacity
- Inventory levels
- Backlog of unfilled orders
- Seasonal factors
- Availability of personnel
- Profit objectives
- Sales objectives
- Customer need for products or services
- Mobilization and progress payments
- Customer financing

5. What information is available regarding prices set by competitors? How are competitors' prices determined or estimated? Has there been or is there any evidence of price collusion in the industry?

6. Is this business a leader and trendsetter in pricing, or does it simply follow or react to competition?

7. What are the usual terms and discounts given on products or services sold?

8. Are there price lists? If yes, obtain date of last revisions and obtain copies. How closely are the price lists followed? Are the lists scheduled for revision?

9. Describe the cost system used in pricing. Are overhead allocations used for each product or service line reasonable, or a source of controversy?

10. Obtain the history of price increases or decreases and the probability of future revisions? Is the business under competitive or customer pressure to decrease prices?

11. How difficult, or easy, can cost increases be passed on as price increases?

12. Is there evidence and/or strong opinions that the business overprices or underprices its products or services?

13. Is this business in an industry with a history of price wars? Are any in progress or threatened?

14. Are any of the products under price pressure from generic or private label brands? Does this business sell and price its products as generic or as private label products?

15. Does this business set or recommend prices for distributors, retailers, or other resellers to sell its products? If yes, review the legality of such practices.

16. What are the policies on returns and restocking?

17. Does the business pay "mark down" money guaranteeing minimum profits if goods prove to be slow moving and difficult to sell? If yes, what is the potential financial exposure?

18. Are distributors and retailers protected from a decline in inventory value if the business reduces prices?

19. Does this business have a department responsible for estimating costs for pricing? If yes, review its performance history, comparing completed jobs to original estimates. To whom does the function report?

20. Has this business been, or is it now, involved in barter arrangements or counter trading? If yes, what have been the results?

21. If financing is provided to customers, how is the cost factored into pricing?

22. Are there clear trends indicating prices may decline or will increase?

23. Are customers required to submit all or a portion of the price upon placing their order? On large contracts, are mobilization and progress payments negotiated? If yes, how does the timing of payments compare with the actual costs of production?

CHAPTER 13
Advertising

PRIMARY ISSUES AND OBJECTIVES

A. Advertising is a challenge to evaluate because results are often difficult to measure. Occasionally, the results are obvious, with increased sales directly attributable to a campaign, but these cases are the exception. Usually, the effect of advertising is not so quick to appear, and only then over a period of time. Without immediate results, controversy may appear in the form of management questioning the quality of the program and the level of expenditures.

B. Advertising varies greatly from business to business in every respect, ranging from little or none to huge programs with multi-million-dollar expenditures. Media advertising, Internet ads, direct mail, trade shows, support for charitable events, and production of collateral material are all possible elements designed to meet specific objectives. Identifying the objectives is a necessary first step in evaluating the expenditures and determining if the objectives are being achieved.

C. Although much of an evaluation of advertising expenditures and results will rest on subjective opinions and observations, reasonable conclusions should be possible.

QUESTIONS AND PROCEDURES

1. Does this business spend funds on advertising? If yes, what was the amount spent last year and the amount planned to be spent this year? Break down expenditures by categories such as media, shows, collateral materials, etc.

2. Obtain copies of advertising budgets and overall plans.

3. In addition to introducing new products or services and increasing sales, what are the objectives of the programs (i.e., improve image, attack competitors, etc.)? Does the business have clearly defined advertising policies and objectives?

4. Have there been any attempts to measure the effectiveness of the advertising program? If yes, obtain copies of the studies or surveys.

5. If the business has multiple business units, is the advertising program centralized, or is each unit largely on its own? If the programs are decentralized, is there any coordination?

6. Identify personnel involved in advertising and their reporting relationships.

7. Identify all advertising agencies utilized and their billings last year and this year to date. How were they selected? If any are on a retainer, what are the terms of the agreement? Are any under consideration for termination, and are new ones being sought. Have any agencies been changed in the past five years?

8. Compare the advertising program to that of major competitors.

9. Identify the media, including all publications, radio, TV, and the Internet, in which the business has advertised during the past two years. What were the expenditures for each?

10. Request copies of advertisements, videos, and collateral literature.

11. Does this business participate in trade shows? If yes, describe importance, cost, and level of participation.

12. Has this business ever been accused of deceptive advertising?

13. List all trademarks, trade names, and logos, and management's estimate of their importance. Are they properly registered or copyrighted?

14. Are the advertising and public relations activities combined under one executive? If not, how are they coordinated?

15. How are advertising expenses recorded in the financial statements, and are the expenses promptly recorded?

CHAPTER 14
Public and Investor Relations

PRIMARY ISSUES AND OBJECTIVES

A. PR—public relations—is a term in common usage, but it covers a wide range of potential activities, making it imperative for any investigator to first determine the activities of the business falling within that category. The activities may be disbursed throughout the organization, or concentrated into a single department managed by an experienced PR executive; it also may be combined with advertising. Financial PR may be totally separate.

B. The public's, customers', and employees' perceptions of the reputation of this business and its management may constitute an invaluable asset or a serious liability. The reputation may not be uniform for all categories, as is illustrated by the possibility that investors might enjoy their return, but the communities in which the business is located have an intense dislike. An investigator can not assume a positive (or negative) reputation in one area will apply to all other areas.

C. Are there programs to enhance positive perceptions and to mitigate those that are negative? Exactly what are the programs, and who is involved? Identify the public relations issues to which most attention is given. Are there neglected PR issues that should be addressed?

QUESTIONS

1. What is the general reputation of this business with investors, shareholders, customer, the community, and employees? Are there any current

PR problems confronting the business that are serious? If yes, what are the causes? Are there any programs to improve relations and image in any of these areas?

2. During the past five years, has this business, its shareholders. or any of its officers received media attention for any reason, favorable or unfavorable? If yes, obtain copies of news articles.

3. Does the business retain a public relations firm or have a relationship of calling a firm when needed? If yes, what is its name, annual billings, function, present assignments, and the length of the relationship?

4. If the business has an internal public relations program, what is its purpose, role, activities, and current projects or assignments?

5. Identify employees involved in public relations and their reporting relationship. Do they have ready access to the CEO? Do they have status and are relied upon by senior management? Are they considered as a separate department? Obtain the resume of the executive in charge.

6. What is the relationship with personnel involved in advertising? Are they the same personnel? Is there a clear understanding as to what constitutes advertising and what is PR? Is there coordination between the two functions?

7. Is political lobbying and government relations part of the PR function? If yes, describe in detail.

8. Are community relations, including contributions and participation in charitable events, part of the PR function? If yes, describe in detail.

9. Obtain a list of all charitable donations made last year and those budgeted for this year. Are relations with community organizations part of the PR function?

10. What has happened, and what would happen, if a serious PR issue occurred? Who would take charge, and who would be involved?

11. Have bloggers been a problem for this business? If yes, what is currently being done to combat the issue?

12. Has the PR firm or employees been asked to perform tasks that they refused or questioned the propriety of such requests? Who arranges elaborate or unusual entertainment for important customers?

13. Are relations with the financial community and organizations part of the PR function? If yes, describe in detail.

14. Who is involved in and/or responsible for the release of financial information? Who meets with analysts, institutional investors, and shareholders?

15. Who prepares the annual and quarterly reports?

16. Who prepares and distributes press releases?

17. Does the business have a separate Investors Relations department or executive responsible for investor relations separate from the PR personnel?

18. Has this business ever been accused of issuing frequent or overly optimistic press releases to influence its share price?

CHAPTER 15

Manufacturing

PRIMARY ISSUES AND OBJECTIVES

A. Manufacturing can best be evaluated by investigators who have had actual experience in manufacturing. Experienced people understand that few manufacturing operations are perfect in every respect, but it is the overall results that are important. Most manufacturing managers are well aware of areas they can improve and are taking action to do so. The primary objective of the study is to determine the role and importance of manufacturing in the business and quantify, but not dwell on, secondary issues. No evaluation is complete without visits to the manufacturing facilities and interviews with their management.

B. The degree that manufacturing capability and performance influences the profitability of the business is an objective in any study. Manufacturing's role may be insignificant, or it may be a dominant factor. Products manufactured in-house in some businesses may represent only a small fraction of total revenues, but for others, in-house manufactured products may account for all revenues. The future role of manufacturing in the business under study in a changing economy will be a critical issue.

C. Globalization has had, and will continue to have, a profound impact upon manufacturing. Competitive pressures from low-cost producers, outsourcing, alternative suppliers, and a myriad of other factors all combine to influence current and future manufacturing decisions. The business's strategy to market manufactured products and remain competitive in the age of globalization is of great importance. During an investigation, strive to learn the most pressing challenges, problems, and severe pressures operating management is experiencing. Particularly important will be competitive pressures, cost reductions, production schedules, and production capacity to coincide with marketing opportunities.

QUESTIONS AND PROCEDURES

1. Identify each manufacturing facility and warehouse, their location, principal activities, and products produced and stored. Request copies of capability reports or brochures describing the facilities.

2. Is each facility a separate profit center, making it possible to determine profitability, or is some other accounting method utilized?

3. Request all internal financial statements and reports for the past two years, including the current year-to-date numbers, for each manufacturing facility or warehouse. Request copies of all internal reports utilized by management regarding output, efficiency, costs, variances, safety, etc.

4. Identify the executives responsible for management at each location and the executives to whom each reports. Request career summaries, and evaluate performance and potential. How long has each been on their job? Are there any current vacancies or known near future terminations?

5. Are products being produced and shipped on schedule? Are any large orders or projects behind schedule? Are any significant cost overruns occurring?

6. What is the overall quality, age, and condition of the machinery and processes used in manufacturing? Is any nearing the end of its life or becoming obsolete? Compare the machinery and processes to competitors. Are any proprietary and/or unique and provide the business with a competitive advantage?

7. What were the total capital expenditures for machinery and equipment or facilities for the past four years? What are planned for the present year and the next two years? Are any in the planning stage or under discussion but not yet approved? Are there any new facilities or machines on order or under construction?

8. How difficult would it be for a competitor to commence manufacturing similar products?

9. Describe the impact globalization and low-cost foreign manufacturing has had upon the business and manufacturing operations. Have changes been made or are contemplated to remain competitive?

10. Describe whatever in-house industrial engineering exists to support manufacturing. How many professionals are employed? Describe their primary activities (i.e., process and machinery design, plant layout, efficiency improvements, etc.).

11. Are the machine tools and equipment in use designed for and limited to a single application, or are they more "off the shelf" with multiple uses?

12. Manufacturing activities can be measured by criteria often not reflected or highlighted in the financial statements. The presence of positive, marginal, or unfavorable data or trends should be investigated. For each category below, determine the present level and the trends.

    a) Production measured in dollars and units per man-hour

    b) Back orders

    c) Scrap, rework, and returns

    d) Variances

    e) Material costs

    f) Wage costs

    g) Down time

    h) Shipments

    i) Inventory levels and composition

    j) Maintenance costs

    k) Employee turnover

    l) Safety record

    m) Overtime level

    n) Warrantee expense and exposure

13. Describe the manufacturing organization, identifying the responsibilities and functions of each major department. Request organization charts. If warehouse management is separate from manufacturing management, obtain separate charts.

14. Identify any critical manufacturing machines or processes dependent upon licenses, leases, or other contracts.

15. Evaluate the effectiveness of the quality control function. What is this business's reputation for quality? Is there a formal quality control manual written? Has ISO 9000 compliance been requested and/or received?

16. What is the average hourly wage of the factory workers? What is the average hourly cost with factory overhead applied? What hourly cost rate is used in determining charges to customers? Compare manufacturing wage costs with competitors.

17. What percentage of total product costs are attributable to wages? Are wage costs considered a significant competitive factor?

18. At what percentage of estimated total capacity is each unit operating? What is the present work week and level of overtime? What capital expenditures would be required to significantly increase capacity?

19. What level of operations is considered necessary to break even at each manufacturing unit?

20. Are freight and transportation costs a significant factor in this business? Does this business have any transportation advantages or disadvantages compared to competitors?

21. If special orders and change orders are a regular part of the business, are all costs captured and the customers charged?

22. What is the backlog of orders? Is the present backlog considered high, low, or adequate? Are manufacturing production schedules based upon sold orders, sales forecasts, required inventory levels, or some combination?

23. Is maintenance and repair adequate? What will this year's expected cost result in and what is the trend compared to prior years?

24. Is labor and service sold to customers as a separate charge? What are the hourly billing rates to customers?

25. Is the sale of parts and/or consumables a significant factor in this business? Compare the profit margin on consumables and parts with original equipment.

26. Are utility costs significant? How do utility costs compare to competitors?

27. Describe, request, and develop opinions of the facility layouts and the flow of work.

28. Has the business relocated or closed any manufacturing operations within the past three years? Are any moves in progress or under active consideration? Are any moves to offshore locations being contemplated and actively studied?

29. Describe and evaluate the inventory, material control, production planning, and scheduling systems. What computers and software systems are used? Is management satisfied with the systems? Are significant changes being considered or in progress? Does the business use bar coding?

30. Who is responsible for completed inventory and warehouses? Where are the facilities located that store finished inventory? Is this a problem being evaluated?

31. What is the impact of seasonal variations in demand upon manufacturing?

32. Describe any special programs and the results to reduce costs, increase efficiency, improve delivery, quality, safety, etc. Are these programs intended to remedy major problems?

33. Is manufacturing management obsessed with direct-indirect labor ratios?

34. What does manufacturing management consider its three greatest strengths and three greatest problems?

35. Is there any evidence of the preponderance of shipments being made at the end of the month, or are months being held open to increase shipments for the period?

36. Normally, how soon after an order is received is the product shipped? Does the business supply customers parts and components on a "just in time" basis?

CHAPTER 16
Purchasing and Outsourcing

PRIMARY ISSUES AND OBSERVATIONS

A. Purchasing, subcontracting, and outsourcing are all essentially the same function, but slightly different connotations have evolved. Purchasing is commonly thought of as the process associated with buying material, parts, and the hundreds of miscellaneous items needed for a business to operate. Subcontracting has come to mean procuring from others components and services that could be manufactured or provided by the business. Outsourcing refers to contracting out products and services previously manufactured or provided in-house. Regardless, they are all similar functions with many of the same issues and problems. In the questions to follow, the term "purchasing" refers to all three varieties of procurement.

B. As a starting point, an investigator should identify the products, materials, and services procured from others. Learn how purchasing decisions are made and evaluate the systems and procedures utilized. How are transactions conducted? Who are the personnel involved? Who is responsible for evaluating and selecting vendors? How are transactions monitored, and who makes the final decisions? Purchasing involves large sums of money, and the opportunity for dishonesty is ever present. The integrity of personnel is difficult to determine and a most delicate subject to pursue.

C. Does the business strive to maximize its profits by fully supporting aggressive procurement programs and policies? In addition to buying wisely, purchasing can be a great source of intelligence on competitors and the industry. Despite the potential impact purchasing can have on profitability, purchasing personnel often do not have the necessary status and authority. The status of purchasing personnel and their authority is a critical issue for study in the investigation.

QUESTIONS AND PROCEDURES

1. What percentage of total revenues is purchased material, components, commodities, products, transportation, and services?

2. What percentage of total revenues of purchased products is complete and ready for resale to customers?

3. Determine and describe the purchasing function and its actual control over purchasing. If the business has multiple locations in which purchasing is conducted, what policies and controls govern each location's activities? Is there a corporate procurement authority, or is each unit on its own?

4. Who is responsible for purchasing, and what is the purchasing organization at each location? To whom does each purchasing executive report?

5. Identify significant new vendors from whom purchases have been made during the past year or will soon be made.

6. Identify any vendors for which, for any reason, there would be strong resistance within the organization to replace.

7. Are there serious unresolved controversies with any suppliers? Identify any vendors with which there is general dissatisfaction.

8. Are there active programs or objectives to aggressively reduce the cost of purchased materials, products, or services? If yes, request copies of reports on the effort or program.

9. If production is scheduled and relies on "just in time" receipt of material, evaluate how well the system is functioning and the reliability of the suppliers.

10. Have long-term supply contracts with vendors been negotiated? If yes, request a list of all the contracts, and review copies of the most important contracts.

11. Does this business enter into forward contracts for the purchase of commodities, such as energy, grain, feed stock, metals, or other commodities? If yes, obtain a list and evaluate all outstanding contracts.

12. Are commodity price fluctuations a serious concern and a risk in this business? If yes, what defensive measures does the business utilize?

13. Identify any vendors with whom automatic electronic reordering agreements are in place. Evaluate the effectiveness of any such arrangements.

14. Describe any sole-source supply situations. Are any of these suppliers at risk because of financial or political instability? Are steps being taken to correct the situation?

15. Describe any unusual or significant purchase commitments existing or soon to be made.

16. Describe any vendor relationships that may involve conflicts of interest. Are any vendors used because senior management or shareholders suggest or require their use? Do any executives or shareholders have a financial interest in any vendors?

17. What is this business's policy with regard to employees accepting gifts and entertainment from vendors? If it is a written policy, obtain a copy.

18. Have any employees been suspected, accused, or discharged for accepting anything of value from vendors during the past five years? Is there any history of kickbacks, excessive gifts, or other valuable benefits given by vendors from whom this business buys?

19. Is this business in an industry where kickbacks, valuable gifts, and expensive entertaining are common?

20. Is purchasing largely the responsibility of one individual with little review?

21. Evaluate the degree of discretion permitted to first-level buyers in selecting vendors and negotiating prices.

22. What are the education levels, experience, and training of employees involved in purchasing? Could they be considered professionals?

23. What controls exist on purchasing decisions and contracting with vendors? Are purchase orders issued before purchase commitments are made? Who is authorized to issue POs? Obtain copies of the business's purchase order form. Are purchase contracts from vendors carefully read? Are standard PO contracts supplemented or modified with side letters for any reason? If yes, who approves the variations?

24. Is there a problem with personnel making purchase commitments and bypassing the purchasing department and established procedures? Are vendor representatives required to first obtain approval of purchasing personnel before meeting with others?

25. Are import tariffs a significant cost factor effecting purchasing decisions?

26. How do vendors view this business? Do any refuse to quote because they believe they have no chance of receiving the order? Are any vendors "black balled" for any reason? Does the business maintain a confidential list of unacceptable vendors?

27. Could this business be adversely affected by fluctuations in commodity prices or currency valuations? If yes, what defensive steps, such as hedging, are taken?

28. How are freight and other transportation services purchased for both incoming products and shipments to customers? Who is responsible? Does the business have highly trained employees involved, or is there a dependence upon outside vendors? Is this a significant cost of doing business?

29. Does this business receive rebates from suppliers? If yes, how are they negotiated, monitored, and recorded?

30. Is this a business engaged in subcontracting or outsourcing of operations, components, products, or services? If yes, describe in detail, including names of vendors, products, or services provided and annual dollar volume. Identify those located in other countries.

31. Is subcontracting or outsourcing a source of controversy within or outside this business? How aggressive and determined is the opposition?

32. Identify any subcontracting or outsourcing of operations, products, or services that, during the past five years, were previously manufactured or provided by the business "in house."

33. Identify subcontracted or outsourced products or services that have never been "in house."

34. Is there a potential for additional subcontracting or outsourcing? Are any possibilities under study or in progress? Have any subcontracted operations, products, or services been returned to "in house" or are under study to be returned?

35. Have any "back office," accounting, product support, or research and development operations been outsourced? If yes, identify each and evaluate the success or failure when compared to the original rational and financial projects.

36. For each subcontractor and outsourcer, obtain an evaluation of their performance. Are any vendors considered unsatisfactory, and are new sources actively being sought?

37. Identify any vendors who have been criticized by this business, either privately or publicly, for labor practices and/or environmental issues? If yes, obtain full details. Is this a serious problem?

38. What is the duration of the contracts with each subcontractor or outsource, and are they likely to be renewed?

39. Does the investor conducting this study have the capability to perform any work or services currently being subcontracted?

CHAPTER 17

Human Resources and Employees

PRIMARY ISSUES AND OBSERVATIONS

A. An investor will want to know the number of employees and their location, as well as identify others who are not classified as employees but are performing services for the business. It is essential to study all categories to understand the true cost of labor because of the increased utilization of contract and temporary employees.

B. The programs and policies of the business relative to employees are of particular importance if the investor has plans to merge work forces. If extreme differences exist, plans that appeared good in theory may be difficult to accomplish in practice.

C. With every work force, there exists problems and challenges. Most are normal and under control, but some are of such serious proportions that they could be "deal killers." Severe labor shortages, safety concerns, excessive turnover, and high labor costs are examples of potential significant problems. Whatever the problems, they should be identified and evaluated.

QUESTIONS AND PROCEDURES

1. Does this business have a human resources department? If yes, how is it staffed and what are its responsibilities? To whom does the senior human resources executive report? Are human resources personnel involved in significant business decisions?

2. What is the number of full-time employees? (Exclude part-time, contract, and temporary employees.) Subdivide the total by country and business

unit in which they are employed. Request lists, if needed, of employee names, job titles, and compensation.

3. What, in each category, is the total number of employees exempt from overtime: sales, administrative, professional and executive employees? Include those legally exempt but still being paid overtime.

4. What is the total number of hourly full-time (nonexempt) employees? Are there seasonal variations? What are the skill levels within this group?

5. What is the total number of employees classified as temporary? Under what circumstances and conditions are employees considered temporary?

6. What is the total number of contract employees, i.e., those working for the business but not on the payroll of the business? Why are contract employees utilized?

7. What is the use and total number of part-time employees?

8. In all the categories of employees listed above, have there been significant increases or decreases during the past year? Are any planned?

9. How many job openings exist in each category of employees? Is there a shortage of employees in any category that adversely affect the operations of the business? Is overtime required because of shortages of employees? Is employee turnover in any category a serious problem?

10. Are any significant layoffs or closings in progress or being contemplated? Have any occurred in the past year?

11. Obtain copies of all personnel manuals, employee manuals, or documents describing benefits, rules, and other terms of employment. Are any of the documents out of date or amended? Can any be interpreted as employment contracts?

12. Determine how employees are recruited and selected at all levels? What are the procedures, techniques, and personnel involved?

13. Are executive search firms utilized? If yes, identify the firms and fees paid. Are any searches in progress?

14. Are psychologists utilized to test job applicants? If yes, identify the psychologists, fees paid, and the type of applicants tested.

15. Identify all employees who have employment contracts and obtain copies. What was the purpose of the contracts? Did the employer or the employees request the contracts?

16. Identify employees who have been required to sign noncompetition agreements and/or confidential information agreements. Identify any who refused to sign. Obtain copies of forms. Has there been any litigation or threatened litigation by or against former or existing employees over the agreements?

17. What training, formal or informal, is provided employees at all levels? Describe the programs. Does the business reimburse employees for tuition for college-level courses? What results and benefits to the business have been identified?

18. Does the business recruit at colleges? If yes, at which colleges, and what has been the success rate? Is there a summer intern program?

19. What are the policies on use of company automobiles and aircraft?

20. What has been the safety record of the business? Describe the safety program and those responsible. Have there been any state or OSHA inspections and, if yes, what were the results? What were the worst accidents in the past 10 years? Has the business ever been fined or prosecuted for safety violations?

21. Are there any occupational health hazards associated with the operation of this business? If yes, obtain full details, including status of litigation or potential litigation. What protective measures are in place to prevent occupational health problems? Are there occupational hazards or health issues common to this industry?

22. What has been the cost of workmen's compensation for the past three years? Is this, or will it likely be, a significant problem area for the business?

23. Obtain a breakdown, by age, of the employees. Is an aging work force a serious present or potential problem?

24. What has been the history and present retirement policy of the business?

25. Has the business had, or does it now have, any programs to encourage or force retirements? If yes, obtain full details of the plans, the cost, and the actual results.

26. What plans are in place, or efforts made, to preserve, transfer, or have access to the knowledge of retiring employees? Are retired employees rehired?

27. Are older job applicants employed? Is there overt or de facto age discrimination? Are job applicants with disabilities employed?

28. Does this business employ minors or illegal aliens? Is this business in an industry known for frequent violations of labor and/or immigration laws? What measures are in place to avoid hiring illegal workers? Does the business recruit highly trained technical personnel in other countries and assist in the immigration process?

29. Are employees given physical examinations prior to employment?

30. What psychological tests are administered to new applicants? Are psychological tests administered to employees being considered for promotion?

31. What is the substance abuse policy? Are employees tested for drugs?

32. What is the policy when employees are found to be alcoholic?

33. Does the business utilize consultants and contract employees on a regular basis? Has their relationship been studied to verify that they should not properly be classified as employees? Could this become a serious issue?

34. What are unemployment compensation costs? Are rates and claims monitored and challenged if questionable? Is this a significant cost factor?

35. Is employee and/or company security a major concern? Do employees travel to or work in areas that are considered dangerous, either because of political instability or disease. If yes, describe precautions taken.

36. Does this business perform work for governments that is classified, and for which employees are required to have government clearance? If yes, what level of security is required, and who is responsible for administration of the system?

37. Does this business have a formal performance review system? If yes, obtain full details. Does the business have a performance review system that involves forced ranking?

38. What has been this business's policies and actual practices regarding employees called to active military duty? Is this a problem area?

39. Have there been any suits or charges of violation of the Wage and Hour or Child Labor laws?

40. Does the business seek compliance of all government regulations and laws and have programs to inform managers of their responsibility?

41. Are any employees required to have government security clearance? If yes, what is the security level? Who is responsible for obtaining clearances and administering the security program?

42. Does the business have programs or retain others to assist terminated employees in finding other employment?

43. Are the employees of this business predominantly of one race, religion, or ethnic origin? If yes, how did this happen? Have there been any clashes or friction between employees because of these differences?

44. Are employees permitted and/or encouraged to work full or part time at home?

45. How does management characterize the overall level of morale?

46. Does the business have a performance review system? If yes, what is its purpose? Does it evaluate employees, improve performance, influence compensation, create a record, etc.? Is a forced ranking system used? Whatever system is in use, is it widely accepted, or has it become a major source of controversy and friction within the organization?

47. Does the business have policies prohibiting nepotism? If not, identify the amount of nepotism that exists. Would this be a serious problem in the

event of a change of ownership? Are any employees on their jobs only because of relationships?

48. Are any employees actively being recruited by competitors?

49. Does the business have a policy of promoting from within whenever possible? Are there systems in place to identify employees qualified for promotion?

CHAPTER 18
Union Issues

PRIMARY ISSUES AND OBSERVATIONS

A. Exploring management's attitude and policies towards unions is essential to learning the true state of labor relations. Their views may range from full acceptance and finding their union helpful in managing the labor force, to open warfare, and anywhere in between. Management's attitude will be a major factor in evaluating the state of their labor relations.

B. If the business has multiple business units with contracts with different unions representing the employees, there may be wide differences in the relations. In one instance, the relations may be excellent, while at another, they may be contentious. Explore the causes of the variance that may be attributed to either management or union policies.

C. The consequences of having organized labor representing employees upon the conduct of the business and how customers may be affected should be explored. Slowdowns and work stoppages delay deliveries and service that customers may tolerate for short periods of time, but not indefinitely. Customers enjoying favorable labor relations with their employees may have little sympathy for vendors who do not.

QUESTIONS AND PROCEDURES

1. List all unions with bargaining rights, their location, and the date their contracts expire. Request copies of the union contracts. If possible, determine when each group was organized and the causes.

2. How does management characterize the state of its relations with its unions? Would this view be similar to those of outside objective observers?

3. Does management expect serious difficulty in negotiating any of its next union contracts? What are the most contentious issues to be negotiated in the next contracts? Does management plan to negotiate any provisions that would reduce present benefits?

4. Who is responsible for negotiating the union contracts? Are the negotiators experienced and objective in labor relations? Does management retain labor attorneys to provide advice on labor issues? If yes, who are they, and what were their billings during the past year?

5. Does the business negotiate its own contracts or is it a part of a multiemployer agreement? If it is part of a multiemployer agreement, does it have a significant voice in the outcome, or does it just accept whatever is negotiated?

6. Do any union contracts contain restrictions on subcontracting or relocating? Has there been vigorous resistance to subcontracting or outsourcing decisions?

7. Are there any ongoing attempts to organize any employees? What has been management's response?

8. List any union representation elections held in the past three years and describe the results. Have there been attempts to organize employees that failed within the past three years and, as a result, elections were not held?

9. List any union decertification elections held or attempted within the past five years. If there were, obtain full details.

10. What has been the strike history at each location?

11. What arbitrations were held within the past 24 months or are scheduled to be held? What is the frequency of grievances being filed?

12. What are the most troublesome aspects of each contract?

13. What is the level of unionization in the industry of which this business is a part? Are major competitors organized?

14. What are the national and local reputations of the unions representing the employees? Have any of the union officers been accused of corruption? Have any union representatives requested any kind of bribe, emolument, or other benefit that may be considered improper? Have any been paid?

15. Have any unfair labor charges been filed against the business in the last five years? If yes, what was the outcome? Are any currently pending?

16. Do any contracts provide supplemental unemployment benefits (SUB)? If yes, what is the duration of benefits? Determine how benefits are funded. What is the present status of the fund? Is this fund's investment policy and record a source of controversy?

17. What benefits are provided to retired employees under the union contracts? What retirement benefits have been negotiated for current employees? How are these benefits funded? What is the condition of the funds, and are they adequate to pay the benefits? Have efforts been made to reduce either pension or health care benefits for retired employees?

18. Does management consult with unions prior to making major decisions affecting the workforce?

19. Are there established grievance procedures for unorganized employees to air their complaints?

20. How does unionization or lack of unionization affect the business's ability to obtain jobs? Is it "double breasted" and able to bid jobs either way? Are union employees used on nonunion jobs? Is this a problem area?

21. Does the business rely upon the union to supply labor?

22. If white-collar and/or professional employees have been organized, determine the causes and how relations have evolved to the present state.

CHAPTER 19
Employee Compensation and Benefits

PRIMARY ISSUES AND OBSERVATIONS

A. There are two primary study objectives: to learn the types of compensation and benefits and their associated cost. Most employee costs are unavoidable if the business is to remain viable. Yet the largest single factor in total employee expense is the number of employees on the payroll, which includes active and perhaps retired employees who still receive benefits. Therefore, the total cost of the business's employees compared to its competitors is a significant area for study.

B. A troublesome problem for any investor is the divergence between compensation and benefits paid within existing controlled businesses and those of the seller. A similar problem exists when comparing community and/or industry compensation costs with the seller's. If the seller enjoys lower costs, the question arises as to how long the cost advantage can continue. If the seller's costs are higher, are there other advantages to offset the difference? Employee expenses have an inexorable tendency to move upward and to the levels of others.

C. Insight into how compensation and benefit levels and programs within the business are determined is essential. Whoever makes recommendations and the process leading to final approvals involves individual managers. Identification of the factors that influence their decisions can be best learned in direct interviews.

D. See Chapter 5, "Directors and Governance," and Chapter 6, "Management," for additional questions relative to the compensation of officers and directors.

QUESTIONS AND PROCEDURES

1. What is the philosophy and policy of the business relative to compensation—to remain competitive within the community, pay higher or lower rates than competitors, etc.? Is there emphasis on performance incentives and goals to determine compensation? What evidence is there that the business knows what others actually pay?

2. How are wage and benefit levels determined, recommended, and approved within the organization? Identify those with authority to approve individual employee's compensation. Identify compensation and benefit consultants retained, their influence, and the amount of their billings during the past year.

3. Are the business's pay scales or rates and benefit costs higher or lower than competitors? Is compensation data exchanged directly with competitors or indirectly through trade associations?

4. Does the business have a formal salary or wage administration plan? If yes, how are jobs ranked and wage levels determined? Are executive level positions included in the plan? Obtain a copy of the plans and/or the wage structure. Are employee evaluations used to influence compensation?

5. What, in total, are employee wage and benefit costs, both in actual dollars and as a percentage of total revenues? What percentage of total labor costs are for benefits?

6. List all retirement plans in effect or announced, including multiemployer plans. Indicate who is covered by each plan. Describe the benefits. Describe the method of funding and annual cost. Is the funding adequate to cover future benefits? Describe in detail the amount of unfunded liability, if any. Obtain copies of the plans or policies, actuarial valuations, trustee reports, and IRS letters of determination. Has there been any litigation, either in progress or threatened by retirees, over benefits? (See Chapter 20 for additional questions.)

7. Are there any plans, either contemplated or in progress, to modify or cancel any benefit programs for existing or retired employees? If yes, obtain full details.

8. What health and life insurance benefits are provided to current or retired employees and their dependents? What is the cost per active employee? What is the cost per retired employee? What portion of the premium is paid by the employee or retiree? Obtain and review copies of the plans and/or policies. Are any of the benefits self-insured by the business? Have any benefits been reduced or employee contributions increased during the past two years? (See Chapter 28 for additional questions.)

9. Identify all profit-sharing plans, and describe in detail who is included and the history of amounts paid. Are these plan benefits a fixed obligation, either as a contractual obligation or by custom?

10. Describe any bonus or incentive plan and who is included. List amounts paid in prior years and those anticipated for the current year. Are these payments contractual obligations, or are they largely at management's discretion? Is it customary to give Christmas or year-end bonuses?

11. Describe any deferred compensation plans in effect and who is covered. List the amounts accumulated and to be paid each participant.

12. Describe any ESOP plans. Obtain copies of the plan and its history. (See Chapter 20 for additional questions.)

13. Describe any stock purchase or savings plans for employees. Obtain full details on participation and costs associated with the plans.

14. Describe any stock bonus or option plans. Obtain copies of the plans and the names of all participants. On what basis are benefits awarded?

15. If the business has a 401(k) plan, obtain a copy of the plan, a list of participants, and the amount of the business's contributions for the past three years. How are the funds invested? What has been the performance of the investments? If shares of the business are in the fund, obtain full details of the amounts and the percent of total funds. (See Chapter 20 for additional questions.)

16. Describe any benefits and the funding source for any terminated or retired employees, such as salary continuation, health and life insurance, club memberships, recreational facilities, transportation, etc. Identify all those receiving such benefits.

17. List all employees who have employment contracts. Obtain copies and summarize each. Determine the purpose of entering into the contracts. Is there reason to believe some employees without written contracts may claim they have a contractual relationship because of policies either written by or verbalized by the business?

18. Describe the business's severance pay policies, practices, and obligations. Will a change of ownership trigger any severance pay obligations?

19. What are the vacation and sick leave benefits? Can these be accumulated from year to year if not taken? If accumulation is permitted, what is the quality of the records? How are these benefits funded and accounted for in the financial statements?

20. Does the business have any full employment or no-layoff policies?

21. Have any benefit plans been introduced, terminated, or modified during the past three years? Have any efforts to modify plans failed because of employee resistance? Describe the effect and/or results of any changes.

22. Create a summary of any benefit and compensation plans and/or agreements that may cease if there is a change in control or ownership of the business.

23. What programs does the business have, if any, to mitigate taxes on options, deferred compensation, stock purchase, stock bonuses, or other similar plans?

24. Has the business made loans to employees at any level? If yes, obtain a list of all outstanding loans or loan commitments and the circumstances for their issuance.

25. Does the business have any "elder care" programs to assist employees in caring for their parents?

26. What is the compensation plan and benefits for employees transferred to or hired to be stationed in foreign countries? What assistance is provided for housing, cost of living, taxes, medical costs, vacation, and travel pay? Are they given extra insurance because of unusual hazardous locations?

27. Does the business offer health savings plans? If yes, what is the level of participation and how is the plan administered?

28. Compare the compensation and benefit plans for executives, managers, and employees to those of other businesses owned by the potential investor.

29. In the past three years, have there been any total or partial wage freezes? Have any segment of employees had their wages cut?

30. Are there any employees whose compensation consists partially or entirely of commission payments based upon performance? If yes, obtain a list of all such employees and the amount of commissions paid to each during the past year and the amount paid year to date. Are any commission employees given a guaranteed draw? Estimate the amount of commissions earned but not yet paid. Obtain copies of any commission plans and/or contracts.

CHAPTER 20

Retirement Plans, 401(k)s, and ESOPs

PRIMARY ISSUES AND OBSERVATIONS

A. Identification of all plans of this type and obtaining the documents creating and supporting the plans should be the first step. Obtaining the names of the participants and those who may become eligible can follow. The purpose of each plan and the associated expense should be evaluated along with the opinions of the participants.

B. The annual present cost and anticipated future costs should be determined and the adequacy of contributed funds analyzed. The ability of the business to absorb the costs is an ever-present factor. The trend of moving away from defined benefit plans to those with fixed annual or even discretional company contributions has accelerated. The avoidance of unfunded liabilities has become popular with management, but not always with employees.

C. Administrative issues and investment decisions can present serious problems. Examples of such concerns include: excessive administrative costs, investments producing substandard returns resented by the fund participants, and an administration that is slow to act, producing unsatisfactory results. Administrative failures of this sort may result in a lack of participation and/or withdrawals by the fund participants.

QUESTIONS AND PROCEDURES

1. List all retirement plans in effect or announced, including multiemployer plans. Obtain copies of each plan and all supporting documents given to

participants or possible participants. Obtain copies of all fund reports, lists of investments, audits, and correspondence with government agencies. How is each plan administered? Identify the administrators and their relationship to the business. Are there any individual plans negotiated for senior executives?

2. Who are the participants in each plan, and what are the benefits? What are the eligibility requirements to participate? What are the vesting schedules? Under what conditions may a participant withdraw from a plan, and how will benefits be affected?

3. How is each plan funded? What has been the annual cost for the past three years and what is anticipated during the next five years? Is funding adequate to cover future benefits? Is there any unfunded past service liability? Are contributions of the business made on a timely basis? Does the business have plans, and is it able to meet all its obligations to the plans?

4. What portion of the cost, if any, do employees contribute? Are employees allowed to vary their contributions and change the amount from time to time? What is the maximum employee contribution?

5. Obtain copies of any actuarial valuations, trustee reports, and IRS letters of determination. What interest assumptions are used by the actuaries?

6. Is there any litigation, actual or threatened, regarding any of the plans? Have any employees expressed dissatisfaction with the plans?

7. Has the business discontinued or revised any existing plans in the past four years? Identify any new plans introduced within the past three years or under consideration to be introduced. If yes, obtain full details.

8. What benefits under any plans are provided to retired employees? Have any of these benefits been recently revised or terminated? What is the annual cost of such programs for retirees, and how are they funded? Is this a serious problem area?

9. If the business has a 401(k) plan, list the participants and the amount of employer contribution for the past three years. Are the employer contributions mandatory or voluntary? What are the employee contributions? What are the eligibility requirements? What is the vesting schedule?

10. For each plan, identify the trust funds or other types of accumulated funds and the following information:

    a) Who has the authority to vote the shares in the plan?

    b) What has been the overall investment performance of the funds?

    c) Who makes investment decisions, and how are they made?

    d) Are any funds invested in shares of the business's securities?

    e) Have any of the investments been to "insiders" or are controversial?

    f) Identify all investments that are not liquid.

g) What is the annual cost of administration and investment advice?

h) What percentage of the funds are charged for administration?

i) Compare the administrative percentage to national statistics.

11. Does the business have an ESOP plan? If yes:

a) Request a copy of the plan and the current share appraisal.

b) What is the plan's history, including why it was established?

c) What was the source of the shares purchased by the plan?

d) Who votes the plan's shares?

e) Compare the plan valuation of the shares with the present market.

f) What are the plans for repurchasing or participants selling their shares?

12. Identify all individuals or organizations that have provided assistance in creating or administering any of the plans, such as attorneys, accountants, appraisers, investment advisors, administrators, actuaries, etc. For each, discover how they were selected, the quality of their performance, and the fees paid.

CHAPTER 21
Culture of the Business

PRIMARY ISSUES AND OBSERVATIONS

A. Culture encompasses all aspects of the relationships between management, employees, customers, and the community. The overall cultural environment in which employees work directly affects the success of the enterprise, and while individual cultural factors can be identified, their importance is difficult to measure. What may appear insignificant to an outside observer may be coveted by the employees, or vice versa. Cultural factors do not readily fit into categories of desirable or undesirable, best or worst, and, except for the most extreme, classification is pointless.

B. Never underestimate the importance of cultural factors in a business. *Neglecting to appreciate cultural differences and efforts to bring about change are leading causes of acquisition failure. Newly appointed senior executives often flounder because of their inability to appreciate cultural factors.* Those attempting to make changes often consider resistance to be irrational, having little sympathy with the opposition; however, they soon discover management edicts are rarely effective solutions. Established cultural factors are difficult to change and may thwart logical schemes to merge operations with grand synergistic savings.

C. Determining the differences between business cultures is critical in any evaluation. Many cultures have simply evolved and represent the policies of founders and various CEOs. However, whatever has survived must enjoy support, however small or formidable. The present CEO's attitude and practices may be one of acceptance of whatever exists or engaged in determined efforts to make changes believed to benefit the business. Discerning the CEO's management philosophy and style will be a key factor in understanding the culture.

QUESTIONS AND PROCEDURES

1. Assume the investor's management philosophy and style are the norm. Identify significant areas of deviation from this norm in the business under study. Review management's style, policies, and approach in dealing with employees, customers, the community, and all others of importance.

2. Have management philosophies resulted in policies and practices that most dispassionate observers would consider to be extreme, excessive, or atypical of customary business practices?

3. Compare the cultural factors of this business with those known to exist in key competitors and in other businesses in the community.

4. Does the business have a mission statement? If yes, is it prominently displayed and followed?

5. Does the business have a code of ethics? If yes, is it well known and followed? Who is responsible for compliance?

6. What is the racial and ethnic composition of management and the work force? Has this been a source of conflict or could potentially be in the future?

7. Is there one prominent religion within management and the work force? Has religious affiliation affected employment or promotions, either overtly or covertly? Are religious activities authorized or tolerated on the property of the business?

8. If the business operates in several countries, how are language and cultural differences recognized and handled? Are there internal conflicts resulting from these issues?

9. What financial information does the business disclose to employees? Is there an effort through disclosure to make employees feel part of the team?

10. Does this business have a culture that encourages innovation or conformity, or a mixture of both? What evidence is there? Are employees at all levels encouraged to voice suggestions and new ideas?

11. Is there a formal or informal dress code?

12. Are employees encouraged to participate in community activities? Are they given paid time off to do so? How does the community view this business?

13. Does management participate in political activities? What is management's attitude towards employees participating in political activities? Is there any evidence of rewards or reprisals for political activity and/or political affiliation? (See Chapter 23, "Government Business, Lobbying and Politics.")

14. Does management promote physical fitness with programs and/or facilities?

15. Does the business have programs and/or policies for maternal leave?

16. Does the business have a policy of mandatory retirement? If not, how are aged long-term employees treated?

17. What are the hours senior executives normally work? Are any devoting less than full time to the business? Do any work long hours to set an informal example?

18. What hours do management and professional employees exempt from overtime normally work?

19. Is this business engaged in any management innovations that are controversial?

20. Does the business retain consultants? If yes, what are their assignments? What is the amount paid during the past year for each consultant? How are their activities received by employees?

21. Describe all training provided by the business, including costs, who is involved, purpose, and results. Does the business reimburse employees for courses at educational institutions?

22. Has the business made investments or purchases from vendors because of social, political, racial or religious considerations?

23. Identify any unusual practices or benefits offered by the business that are coveted by the employees.

24. Identify any unusual practices or policies of the business that most employees find offensive.

25. Are there employee clubs or organizations?

26. Does the business provide recreational facilities for employees? Are some facilities limited to certain classes of employees?

27. Identify all women in senior management. Do women believe they have opportunities for advancement?

28. What are the decision-making and approval procedures for making charitable contributions? Is there a donation and contribution budget? If yes, obtain a copy. What was spent last year, and what is budgeted for this year?

29. Identify large shareholders or key officers who influence the business's decisions regarding charitable contributions. Identify the organizations they support in which they are active, and the offices held.

30. Obtain a list of the actual donations made to each organization during the past year. How dependent upon the business's contribution are these organizations?

31. Are employees pressured to donate to any charitable organizations?

32. Does the CEO or the spouse give strong support to any charity?

33. Has the business ever made contributions to a religious organization, either presently or in the past five years? If yes, obtain the amounts and learn the circumstances.

34. Are employees given time off with pay to participate in charitable events?

CHAPTER 22
Legal and Regulatory Issues

PRIMARY ISSUES AND OBSERVATIONS:

A. Identification of potential, or existing, legal and regulatory conflicts requires great care, since their existence can have such a profound impact on the value and future of the business. In almost all businesses, some issues of this type exist.

B. All issues identified must be evaluated as to probable outcome, with cost parameters estimated. Unfortunately, the final outcome in many cases will not be known until a settlement or decision occurs, until such time estimates will have a large element of uncertainty. The quality of estimated settlement parameters is influenced by the experience and judgment of those making the estimates. Due diligence regarding regulatory issues and litigation requires the assistance of attorneys.

C. The business's philosophy and attitude towards government regulations and litigation should readily become apparent while interviewing executives. Do they allow emotions and prejudices to outweigh good business judgment, or do they make calculated decisions in the best interest of the business? Are they quick to file suits, settle when possible, fight most suits, or file countersuits of dubious merit? Do they accept government regulations and try to comply, or do they attempt to circumvent or ignore regulations they believe are detrimental to the business? Discerning the philosophy of management and whether it is at variance with that of the investor is critical in the study.

QUESTIONS AND PROCEDURES:

1. Identify all executives and employees involved in handling legal and regulatory matters. Describe the in-house legal function. What type of

work is handled in house, and what is assigned to outside attorneys? Who assigns legal work? Identify all in-house attorneys.

2. What outside law firms and/or attorneys are used by the business? Identify the type of cases or issues assigned to outside attorneys. What were the business's legal expenses for each of the past three years? Itemize amounts paid to each firm and/or attorneys.

3. Does the business have in place procedures to keep management and employees informed of new or existing federal and state legislation or areas of expanding litigation, such as sexual harassment, wrongful discharge, workplace discrimination, family leave, rights of employees called to military service, and obligations to the handicapped? Who in the business is responsible for compliance?

4. Obtain details on all claims, actions, suits, arbitrations, investigations, disputes, or other proceedings against the business, pending, threatened, or anticipated. Review all relevant pleadings, documents, and files. Interrogate all employees and attorneys involved. Estimate legal costs, date of resolution, and amount, if any, of loss. Segregate those insured from the uninsured. If insured, is the coverage adequate, and does the carrier accept the claim?

5. Obtain details on all claims, actions, suits, arbitrations, investigations, disputes, or other proceedings by the business, pending or anticipated, against others. Review all relevant pleadings, documents, and files. Interrogate all employees and attorneys involved. Estimate legal costs, date of resolution, and probable amounts recovered, as well as the terms of the settlement.

6. Are there any possible terms of the resolution of any of the conflicts identified in points 4 and 5 above, either by the business or against the business, that could materially affect the future conduct and/or the financial health of the business?

7. Currently or within the past five years, has the business or any of its officers or directors been subject to any fine, penalty, order, writ, injunction, restraining order, settlement agreement, or decree of any court, department, agency, or instrumentality? If yes, has there been any default? Request copies of all the relevant documents.

8. Request a copy of all settlement agreements relating to any suit, action, claim, arbitration, investigation, dispute, or other proceeding either by or against the business that is in the process of being settled or has been settled within the past six years. Are there any settlements that restrict any operations of the business? Are the terms of any settlements secret?

9. What is the business's usual reaction when threatened or actually sued? When suits are threatened or filed, how are they evaluated and processed?

10. Is this business quick to file lawsuits against others? Are suits used to intimidate competitors or others? Who makes the decision on when to file a suit?

11. What reserves have been established for potential litigation losses? Evaluate their adequacy. Has the business booked income in anticipation of a favorable outcome of litigation, although actual cash has not been received? It yes, obtain full details.

12. Request a copy of all letters sent during the past three years from attorneys representing the business to the business's independent auditors concerning litigation or any other matters.

13. Describe in detail any past, current, or anticipated litigation against any officers, directors, or major shareholders for activities related to the business. Is there any well-publicized litigation in progress against any of these individuals over issues unrelated to the business?

14. Has the business or any of its major shareholders, directors, officers, or key employees been charged with criminal activities?

15. Describe all claims, actions, suits, arbitrations, or other proceedings brought by shareholders of the business, pending, threatened, or anticipated, against any director or officer of the business.

16. Describe any claim against, or liability of, the business on account of product or service warranties or with respect to the manufacturing, licensing, sale, or rental of defective products. Is there any basis for such claims? Are the claims insured?

17. Have there been any investigations or inquiries by the Consumer Product Safety Commission or by any other federal, state, or local agency or government entity with respect to products manufactured or sold by the business, or with products that are similar or of the same type as products manufactured by the business?

18. Detail all pending worker's compensation claims and all such significant claims that have arisen in the past three years. Is the business aware of any events or hazardous conditions with the potential to cause a significant increase in insurance premiums?

19. Describe any claim, action, suit, investigation, dispute, or proceeding against the business, pending, threatened, or anticipated, relating to any violations or alleged violations of any laws, rules, or regulations. Give particular attention to those relating to: taxes, the environment, occupational safety and health, foreign corrupt practices, sexual harassment, age, racial or other types of discrimination, wage and hour laws, the handicapped, child labor laws, and employment of aliens.

20. Has the business complied with all laws and regulations and orders of regulatory agencies relating to the operation of the business? During the past three years, has there been any action taken by a government entity against the business? If yes, what was the outcome?

21. Describe all suits, claims, disputes, or other proceedings involving the infringement or alleged infringement of any of the business's permits, licenses, franchises, certificates, trademarks, trade names, patents, patent applications, copyrights, drawings, schematics, designs, or similar proprietary and/or intangible rights. Describe all action that the business is taking to stop such infringement.

22. Describe any claims, suits, disputes, or other proceedings, actual or threatened, by the business involving allegations of infringements of intellectual property rights.

23. Has the business or any agent of the business, directly or indirectly, within the past five years, given or accepted any gift or similar benefit to or from any customer, supplier, or government employee or other person in a position to help or hinder the business, which: 1) might result in damages or penalties in any civil, criminal, or government proceeding; or 2) if not continued in the future, might materially and adversely affect the assets, business operations, or prospects of the business?

24. Has the business or any of its employees been charged with price-fixing, kickbacks, market splitting, or payoffs? Has the business ever been the subject of any government agency investigations regarding these activities?

25. Is this business in an industry or operating in a state or country where price-fixing, bid rigging, market splitting, kickbacks, or payoffs are known to occur? Does the business operate in any states or countries with a reputation for corruption?

26. If this business belongs to any trade associations, how are these associations kept free of illegal activities by members? Have any been accused of improper activities?

27. Does the potential investor and the business operate in any of the same markets? Are there any foreseen antitrust concerns if the investor acquires this business?

28. If the business has made any acquisitions within the past 10 years, are there any disputes with selling shareholders for any reason? If any purchases involved an earn-out, has it been concluded, or is it yet to be settled?

29. Regarding the business or any of its assets, divisions, or subsidiaries, what contractual obligations of the business or with former owners survive?

30. Are there any disputes with former officers or employees? If yes, learn details.

31. Are there any trends, events, or litigation in the business's industry that would indicate the business may become the subject of substantial litigation? Does the business have insurance to cover this eventuality?

32. Are there any proposed changes in legislation or government regulations that would have a material effect upon the business?

33. Is the business in compliance with Sarbanes-Oxley?

34. Determine the status of each suit either by or against the business. Classify into one of the following:

- Suit threatened or probable
- Suit filed
- Discovery not scheduled
- Discovery and depositions complete
- In negotiations or mediation
- Settlement offers made
- Settlement offers accepted or rejected
- No trial date set
- Trial scheduled
- Trial concluded and in negotiations or appealing

CHAPTER 23
Government Business, Lobbying, and Politics

PRIMARY ISSUES AND OBSERVATIONS

A. Business from governments comes in the form of contracts, grants, and subsidies. Contracts are awarded for products, projects, or services and with little concern as to what happens to the business upon completion. Grants are usually in the form of cash awards in response to proposals submitted. Subsidies result from political decisions and are subject to change. A study of government business should determine the nature of contracts in hand, emphasis on the duration of the contracts, the probability of future business, and impact upon the business if additional contracts or grants are not received. Any business dependent upon government funding has risks that most nongovernment businesses do not experience. The task is to determine the importance of government contracts to the business.

B. Only a small percentage of government contracts or grants are awarded on an unsolicited basis without competitive bids or negotiations. However, in recent years there has been an increase in contracts negotiated without competitive bids, and many have proved highly controversial. Regardless of the origin or type of contract, a business must have a system and personnel for aggressively pursuing, negotiating, and administering the contracts or grants. Understanding the government systems, regulations, and skills in writing proposals are often essential for success. Identifying all employees and nonemployees involved is a critical area for study. The possibility of political influence affecting the award of a contract may be claimed or suspected, although it is not a factor in most contract awards. The appropriate contracting government agencies negotiate and award contracts, not the politicians.

If political influence is a factor in the award of contracts, then the source and motivation becomes an important area of study. The motivation can range from impressing the voters with "bringing home the bacon," to highly illegal "quid pro quo" arrangements. The elected officials or agency employees as sources should be identified, their motivation understood and quantified, and the nature and extent of the influence provided. Influence can be exerted in a variety of forms, letters, phone calls, private conversations, and social interaction. Whatever the method or combination of methods, the results are the measure of effectiveness. However, in some instances, the actual effectiveness of the influence may never be known.

C. The degree of political involvement by officers, directors, executives, and employees requires study because it can affect the conduct of the business and may constitute an important factor in its culture. Are individuals involved in politics because they believe it may benefit the business, are they motivated by political convictions, or both? Are employees' careers affected by their political activity or beliefs? Politics produces strong opinions and often little respect for those not sharing the same beliefs.

QUESTIONS AND PROCEDURES

1. What percentage of this business's total revenues are from sales, either directly or as a subcontractor to governments or agencies thereof? Determine the percentage of government business for each division or subsidiary of the business.

2. Identify the products or services sold to government entities, domestic or foreign, either directly or as a subcontractor to others.

3. Are the products or services sold standard with little or no modification, or are they designed to meet government specifications?

4. Identify all outstanding contracts and grants directly linked with government entities, and make a note of such details as the name of the entity, the contract amount, completion date, and present status. What is the probability of additional contracts?

5. Identify all outstanding contracts for products or services with a sub-contractor where the final customer is a government entity. What is the contract amount, completion date, and present status? What is the probability of additional contracts?

6. Are any contracts with government entities or as a subcontractor behind schedule? Are any in trouble, with cancellation a possibility? What would be the impact upon the business if any contracts were cancelled or not renewed?

7. Are any government contracts being renegotiated or subject to renegotiations?

8. Name the governments and/or their contractors with whom the business has contracts or has had contracts within the past three years. For each contract, identify the point of sale and the individual or individuals responsible for the awards.

9. Identify all business currently being pursued or negotiated with any government, government agency, or subcontractor. Obtain full details on each contract, including the name of the buyer, the point of sale, the timing of the award, and the probability of success.

10. Identify significant government business that is anticipated but is not available for bidding or negotiation. Estimate the probability of receiving this business and the timing for the contract awards.

11. Identify contracts being audited by a government agency. Have any audits been conducted or are in progress that have, or may reach, conclusions detrimental to the business?

12. Identify contracts received on a competitive bid basis and those negotiated without bidding.

13. For each contract, review the marketing and selling process. Identify all personnel involved. For each government agency or subcontractor, identify their decision process and what individual or group made the buying decision.

14. Identify any government contracts in which political influence was involved either directly or indirectly in the awards. Identify the elected officials or agency heads who gave assistance. How important was the influence exerted in the award of the contracts?

15. Identify contracts that result from grants. Segregate those contracts in which follow-on grants are probable.

16. Identify any government regulations in existence that are particularly troublesome for the business. What is the level of enforcement?

17. Identify all personnel employed by the business whose primary duties are to obtain government contracts. Identify those involved in administering government contracts. Identify those who previously were elected to government positions or held jobs in government agencies.

18. Identify all consultants, lobbyists, or other individuals and organizations that have or will receive compensation for obtaining information and securing government contracts. For each, identify the services performed, the results, and the amounts paid.

19. Does the business maintain an office in Washington, any state capitals, or foreign countries? If yes, describe the staff, the annual cost, the primary purpose, and the results to date.

20. Identify any elected officials that have been helpful to this business. Is any portion of this business's income dependent upon any individual remaining in office or being replaced?

21. Identify elected officials or agency executives to whom assistance was requested but refused or failed to respond. Are there elected officials or government agencies that have negative views regarding the business or any of its officers or directors? Have any "blackballed" the business?

22. Has this business made political contributions, either in cash or in kind, within the past three years? If yes, learn the amounts, the recipients, the method of contribution, and the purpose. Were the contributions to individuals, parties, or events? Who approved the contributions?

23. Does this business contribute funds to trade associations or other third parties with the expectation that the funds will be used for political purposes? Identify the third parties and the amounts contributed.

24. Does the business make political contributions in kind such as provide transportation, employees to assist, printing, facilities, etc.? Identify the extent and nature of any such contributions.

25. Identify any key shareholders, officers, or directors that are purported to have close relations or ready access to any elected officials or senior appointed officials. Identify those that have made significant personal and political contributions, and identify the recipients.

26. What has been the purpose of political contributions and actual or anticipated benefits to the business?

27. Have political contributions by the business or individuals closely associated with the business been made in accordance with federal and state laws governing such contributions? Has there been an effort made to educate individuals on compliance?

28. Are most or all members of management affiliated with the same political party or share similar political opinions? If yes, does this affect their business decisions?

29. Have any key shareholders, officers, or directors either held or presently hold elective office or been appointed to any commissions or other government agency?

30. Do any key shareholders, officers, or directors hold an office in any political party? If yes, obtain details.

31. Does this business have a political action committee (PAC)? If yes, describe its function, method of raising funds, and list contributions to candidates or causes to date. How are decisions made as to candidates or causes to support?

32. What is the business's policy or attitude towards employees engaging in political activity? Has the business ever actively supported political activity by employees or discouraged political activities in which management was not in sympathy?

33. Is all or any portion of this business's continued operations subject to the renewal or continuance of any government permits or licenses? Obtain a list of all permits, licenses, consents, orders, or authorizations from government or regulatory agencies. Are all current? When does each expire?

34. Is any portion of the business dependent upon government subsidies or grants?

35. Is there any indication that a change in government policies could have an adverse or positive effect upon the business? Give particular attention to tariffs, boycotts, environmental regulation, regulation enforcement, and energy availability.

36. Do any contracts require security clearances? If yes, what level of clearance is required? Who administers the security program to assure compliance?

37. Has the business employed within the past five years any former elected officials or senior agency executives? If yes, what are their present positions and the circumstances that prompted their employment?

38. What is the business's policy on employees called to military service?

39. Identify all employees involved in administering government contracts. Who completes required reports? Who interfaces with government employees? Is administration a problem area?

CHAPTER 24
Information Systems

PRIMARY ISSUES AND OBSERVATIONS

A. Information systems technology is evolving so rapidly that any study involves seeking the answers to three basic questions: What are the systems in use today? Are present systems working well, secure, and adequately serving the needs of the business? And what are today's costs, and can they be justified for state-of-the-art technology?

B. As a result of rapidly changing technology and its impact upon business, management structures have evolved to evaluate, select, and administer the information systems. These structures depend largely upon the size of the business and range from one or two people to large departments overseen by senior executives. The authority of personnel involved and their ability becomes a major factor in any study.

Exactly how new systems are evaluated with costs compared to benefits is an area for study. In addition to the cost of hardware and software, are the costs of administrative and operational support, including training, support, downtime, staffing, maintenance, infrastructure, and installation, recognized?

C. The compatibility of information systems with those of a potential investor can prove to be a serious problem. Often large savings predicted through standardizing and consolidating systems may be difficult to achieve because of a lack of compatibility. Long-term leases and licensing restrictions may further complicate any transition.

QUESTIONS AND PROCEDURES

1. Who is responsible for information systems in this business? Determine the extent of this person's responsibilities and authority in managing or

monitoring systems; approving the internal development, purchase, or lease of all system hardware and software; evaluating new systems; and recommending or rejecting their acquisition.

2. Does this business have an overall strategy relative to information systems?

3. If no one individual is responsible, how are decisions made to acquire hardware, software, and install systems?

4. Request a list of all information systems utilizing computers and their function in the business. List the type of machines, software, their age, number, and location of units.

5. What is the policy on the issuance of mobile IT equipment to employees? Obtain a list of all mobile equipment and to whom it is issued. How is this equipment updated? Is the equipment restricted to business use?

6. Identify software either purchased or licensed from others and software developed within the business that is the property of the business. Identify any software developed from a purchased source code. Identify systems or software purchased from others but modified in house.

7. Does the IT function have a separate budget? If yes, obtain a copy. What percentage of the budget is for existing operations? What percentage is for the development or acquisition of new systems?

8. Identify any IT employees who have exceptional ability to troubleshoot existing systems, enhance systems, or create new systems.

9. Does the business have valid licenses for each system of software? Are there restrictions on transferring any licenses in the event of a change of control of the business?

10. Does the business use vendor financing? Identify all information system hardware, software, and systems that are leased and the terms of the leases. What are the penalties for cancellation?

11. What new information systems are scheduled to be added or to replace existing systems?

12. Identify the systems for which management is most satisfied.

13. Identify the systems for which management is dissatisfied. What corrective measures are being taken or planned?

14. Who is responsible for system support and security? Have viruses and other system breaches been a problem? What security systems and practices are in place to protect the systems?

15. Has the business been a victim of fraud or theft by offenders using the information systems? If yes, what were the circumstances and outcome? Are all mobile IT devices recovered when employees terminate?

16. Do employees have portable IT devices laden with corporate data? If yes, have any been lost or stolen?

17. Have any employees stolen or taken with them corporate data? Is the amount of information and database access limited on mobile equipment?

18. Have any employees had virus-infected IT devices that inadvertently infected the business's host system?

19. Has the business entered into any service contracts? If yes, what are the terms and penalties for cancellation?

20. Have any major new systems been installed within the past year? If yes, why were they installed, and have they worked as planned? Overall, what has been the success in installing new systems?

21. Does the business have a strategic plan with objectives to coordinate, integrate, and standardize information systems? If yes, obtain a copy. Are new systems acquired consistent with the plan?

22. Does the business have a central database? What are the restrictions on access to the database? Describe the extent of networking within the business.

23. Has the business contracted out departments or functions of its information systems? Does the business use service bureaus or contract out software development? Identify the contractors and any consultants and evaluate costs, benefits, and level of satisfaction with their performance. Obtain copies of their contracts and the amount paid each in the past 12 months.

24. What are the backup and disaster recovery procedures and programs?

25. Has the business conducted or arranged for any studies to determine if the cost of any systems has been offset by cost reductions or increases in productivity? If yes, obtain copies.

26. Are there any employees involved in information systems whose departure for any reason would seriously impair the systems?

27. Identify those employees thought to have exceptional skills in writing software, developing systems, or troubleshooting problems.

28. Does the business use any special telecommunications systems to communicate with employees and customers nationwide and internationally? Is this equipment owned or leased?

29. Is teleconferencing commonly used for meetings?

30. If a systems manual has been written for the business, obtain a copy. Is it maintained, up to date, and followed?

31. What hardware is issued to employees for personal use, such as portable computers, cell phones, Blackberries, etc.?

32. Do any employees work full or part time from their homes utilizing information systems? If yes, describe the nature of the work and its effectiveness.

33. How does the business dispose of its obsolete and discarded hardware?

34. Identify the business's Web sites. What is their purpose, and who is responsible for content and maintenance?

CHAPTER 25
Internet

PRIMARY ISSUES AND OBSERVATIONS

A. In only 10 years, the Internet has had a profound global effect upon businesses and how business is conducted. How the Internet has changed business, present applications, and plans or possible uses for utilization in the future are primary questions for this study. To fully answer these questions, investigators will require the assistance of individuals sophisticated in information technology.

B. Businesses continue to find more applications with the evolution of the Internet. Does management aggressively seek new applications to fully exploit the Internet's potential?

C. Any study of a business's use of the Internet should include an evaluation of how present applications are functioning. Are systems in place to accurately process information received over the Internet to the full satisfaction of customers? Identify any problems associated with the Internet and whatever corrective measures are in progress.

QUESTIONS AND PROCEDURES

1. What percentage of total revenues results from sales over the Internet? Compare the volume this year with the volume last year.

2. Identify by product or service the percentage of orders received over the Internet. What is the normal length of time between receipt of an order and shipment?

3. Describe the marketing and advertising programs that utilize the Internet and the cost and effectiveness of the programs. What was the amount spent on Internet advertising during the past year?

4. What has been the purpose and results from the business's Web page?

5. What controls are in place to protect the privacy of customers who place orders over the Internet? Have there been any security problems?

6. Who has been and is responsible for installing, diagnosing, correcting problems, and maintaining systems utilizing the Internet?

7. Describe the department or organization responsible for processing incoming orders. Are there any significant problems?

8. Describe any technical support activities provided through the Internet. Determine the extent of this service and who is responsible. What is the cost of technical support?

9. How serious has the problem been with viruses, hackers, and other disruptive systems attacks? What defensive systems are in place, and have they been effective? Does the business have a program for rapid response to disruptions? Have any systems been shut down or damaged by these attacks? Who does the business have to develop and install defensive software and respond to attacks? Could this business survive if its systems were disrupted for any prolonged period of time?

10. Describe the extent of the use of the Internet as a means of internal communication.

11. What internal controls or policies exist to restrict employee use of the Internet for personal use or entertainment? Has this been a problem?

12. What plans does the business have to expand or improve the use of the Internet? Who is responsible for implementing the plans?

13. How does the Internet fit into the business's overall information technology program? Is one individual responsible for all technology and information systems operations?

14. Compare the business's use of the Internet with that of competitors. Does either enjoy an advantage? If yes, how long will it last?

CHAPTER 26
Budgets

PRIMARY ISSUES AND OBSERVATIONS

A. Past and present budgets should be a primary target of any business investigation. Budgets are internal financial statements and projections prepared by managers to reflect the plans and objectives of the business for the coming year or longer periods. They constitute important management tools prepared primarily for internal use, and not as sales documents designed to influence outside investors. If budgets are used to influence share prices or investors, their integrity should be suspect. Budgets normally contain substantial details of anticipated expenses and revenues not found anywhere else. They can provide greater insight into the condition of the business and management's expectations than any other documents.

B. Budgets of prior years, when compared to actual results, best illustrate in financial terms the successes, failures, changes in direction, new circumstances, and disappointments of management. Every effort should be made to obtain the budgets, although management may be reluctant to permit their release because of possible embarrassment. A comparison of actual results with prior budgets will provide an opportunity to judge their quality and estimate the efficacy of current budgets.

C. The quality of budgets is a reflection of the quality of management. Budgets are such an established proven management tool that the care with which they are constructed and administered is a factor in any evaluation of management.

QUESTIONS AND PROCEDURES

1. Does the business have budgets covering all segments of the business? Identify any segments not included in the budgets. When was budgeting first introduced into the business?

2. Request copies of the present budget and copies of the budgets for the past three years. Compare budgets to actual results and obtain information on significant deviations. Emphasis should be on a comparison of year-to-date results with the present budget.

3. Determine the process through which budgets are constructed. Who is responsible for developing the budget? Identify all individuals participating in the budgeting process. Are executives experienced and sophisticated in creating and managing budgets? Are budgets an important management tool, and is the process taken seriously by all levels of management?

4. What is the philosophy or attitude of those preparing budgets? Are they realistic, conservative, easily attainable, or fantasy? Has senior management conveyed a philosophy as to the type of budget expected?

5. Does senior management establish objectives with those constructing the budgets expected to produce budgets showing how the objectives will be achieved? Is the budgeting process an open discussion in which varying views can be explained, new concepts can be presented, and senior management can learn as well as make suggestions and give final approvals?

6. Does achieving or exceeding budgeted objectives directly affect line managers' compensation?

7. What is the timing for completion of a budget for the next fiscal year?

8. Who is responsible for monitoring the budget during the year? Are managers expected to conduct operations in accordance with their budgets, and are explanations of deviations demanded?

9. Is the budget reviewed and modified during the year as results materialize and circumstances change?

10. How is budgeting coordinated with overall strategic planning? Are those involved in planning an integral part of the budgeting process?

11. Have any budgets been shown to security analysts or potential investors as part of a program to influence the price of shares or to sell the business?

CHAPTER 27
Planning

PRIMARY ISSUES AND OBSERVATIONS

A. Exactly what are the owners' or controlling shareholders' plans for continuing operations of the business? Their plans may be well known or concealed, or they may not have any plans other than maintaining the business as is. Owners' plans do not always coincide with operating management's thoughts on the future of the business, and the views of both should be explored.

B. Strategic planning remains a primary task and responsibility of the CEO. Planning executives or departments may assist in identifying opportunities and making recommendations, but the final result will be the decision of the CEO, and it will be his plan. Yet brilliant, well-conceived plans are only the first step, and many times they can fail during implementation, which is often the stage of greatest challenge for any CEO. The quality of the plan devised and its implementation will weigh heavily in evaluating the success or failure of the CEO.

C. Whether the plan for the future of the business is written and highly formalized, or only in the CEO's head, some sort of plan must exist. The plan may be highly innovative, taking the business in new and often risky directions. The plan could largely be a necessary reaction to present conditions, or simply a plan to continue the business as it now operates. Whatever the plan, an investor must evaluate it and decide if all or part will be continued.

QUESTIONS AND PROCEDURES

1. Does the business have a written strategic plan delineating both short- and long-range objectives? Has the plan been approved by the board of

directors? Has its content been made known to shareholders, investors, and employees? If available, obtain a copy.

2. Does the CEO have a strategic plan that, while not written, is fairly specific and has been made known to others?

3. Have any significant changes in the strategic plan been made within the past two years, and are any being contemplated? Is the plan revised as conditions change, or is it "fixed in concrete"?

4. Whether the plan is formal or informal, is it being followed? How long has the plan been in existence? Is the plan respected, or is it controversial? Is planning considered an important function of the business?

5. Does the business have a mission statement? If yes, is it prominently disseminated and followed?

6. Does the business have an executive responsible for planning? If yes, what exactly are his job duties and the extent of his responsibilities? Other than evaluating the potential of existing business segments and evaluating promising new business opportunities, in what other categories of activities is he involved? To whom does this executive report?

7. What is the planning process, and who are the individuals involved? Has the process been formalized? Is planning strictly a corporate headquarters activity, or are operating divisions and subsidiaries involved in constructing plans?

8. To what degree are the planning activities meshed or coordinated with the budgeting process? Is planning organizationally separate from budgeting?

9. Is the strategic plan reviewed only at regular intervals, or is it under continuous review with frequent changes?

10. Is the business closely monitored by the CEO and/or owners for compliance with the overall plan to achieve both short- and long-range objectives?

11. Overall, does this business have an active planning program that has made a significant contribution to the business? Obtain the opinion of the CEO.

12. Are any changes in the planning process underway or being contemplated?

13. Are planning personnel involved in seeking, evaluating, and negotiating acquisitions? If yes, identify the personnel and their respective roles.

14. If there is an executive department assigned to planning, what has been its history? Has its status changed from time to time, and has there been frequent turnover of personnel?

CHAPTER 28
Insurance and Bonding

PRIMARY ISSUES AND OBSERVATIONS

A. What insurance and bonding does this business presently have in force? What coverage does it not have, and what is the claims experience? Fundamental management decisions requiring considerable judgment are necessary in selecting the type of insurance, the amount of coverage, and the exposure by remaining uninsured. The certain costs of insurance have to be weighed against the uncertain costs of probable risks. The quality of the insurance carriers and their ability and willingness to pay claims are factors not to be overlooked.

B. Performance bonds are issued on the basis of the financial strength of the business and its history of defaults or freedom from defaults. If performance bonds are required in the business, the ability to obtain bonds and the default record becomes an important area of study. Performance bonds usually require guarantees in case of default, and who provides the guarantee in case of an ownership change may become a critical issue. Fidelity bonds are issued to protect against losses from theft or other improprieties perpetrated by employees. Usually they can be readily obtained if the business does not have an unsatisfactory history. Many fidelity bonds require the business to prosecute in order to collect on the bonds, which often presents management with difficult decisions.

C. Insurance and performance bond contracts are often voluminous, complex, and difficult to comprehend. For an investor to fully understand the insurance coverage, an expert on insurance will be needed for the evaluation.

QUESTIONS AND PROCEDURES

1. Request a copy of all insurance contracts in effect. Compile a list of all coverage, amounts, deductibles, premiums, carrier names, and policy expiration dates.

2. Identify all risks where coverage is lacking.

3. Are any policies about to expire with renewal refused, difficult, or at greatly increased premium cost?

4. Who is the insurance broker for the business? How are the carriers selected? Is there competitive bidding? Have any major carriers been changed within the past two years? What were the reasons for the change? Is active consideration being given to changing any of the existing carriers?

5. Are any policies on a retrospective basis? Is any significant income anticipated from favorable experience?

6. Have any carriers cancelled or refused to renew policies in the past three years?

7. Obtain a list of all claims filed against the business by categories of insured, self-insured, and uninsured. Have there been major losses under any policy in the past three years? Identify the claims that were disputed or unpaid. Identify claims that were disputed with the claimant and/or those disputed because the carrier is refusing coverage. What potential financial exposure does the business have from disputed claims?

8. Is the business self-insured in any areas? If yes, secure full information, including the rationale, loss experience, adequacy of reserves, bonding, umbrella policies, or other catastrophe coverage.

9. Does the business provide health insurance for its employees? What percent of the total premium is paid by employees? Is there dependent coverage? What is the annual cost to the business per employee? How does this compare with competitors?

10. Does the business use a health advocacy service to assist and advise the business and employees on health insurance issues?

11. Is the business required to provide bid and/or performance bonds? Is securing bonds a problem? What is the business's bonding limit? Within the past five years, has the business ever defaulted, resulting in a claim filed against the bonding company?

12. Is bonding of employees required? Have there been any fidelity losses?

13. Is the business presently having difficulty in seeking new insurance or bonding?

14. Does the business carry director's and officer's liability insurance? If yes, what are the amounts of coverage?

15. Does the business carry key person life insurance? If yes, who is insured, who are the beneficiaries, and what was the purpose for buying the insurance? What is the present cash value? Has the business borrowed against the insurance?

16. Does the business carry flood insurance? Has flooding ever occurred, and is there a risk flooding may occur? Are any properties in the 100-year flood plain?

17. Are any of the carriers with whom the business has insurance rumored or reported to have financial difficulties that could limit their ability to pay claims? Does the business seek financial ratings on carriers before placing insurance contracts? (The A.M. Best Company provides ratings on insurance carriers.)

18. Were there reasons for selecting any of the carriers other than their quality and competitive rates? Were there factors, such as personal relationships with shareholders or officers, loans to the business, individuals, or ownership of suppliers to or customers of the business? Have there ever been any known or suspected improprieties with carriers?

19. What services do the carriers provide in conjunction with their insurance, such as safety and facility inspections?

CHAPTER 29
Environmental and Safety Issues

PRIMARY ISSUES AND OBSERVATIONS

A. Identifying and quantifying environmental hazards is an essential part of every due diligence investigation, often resulting in many investments being delayed or cancelled. It is difficult to be certain all hazards have been identified, but it is even more difficult to estimate the full cost of remedial measures. Often the full cost will never be known until the remedial work is complete, and that may be years away. Costs may be greater than the value of the business if the hazards did not exist. The costs also become the financial responsibility of the investor if responsibility for the damage or remedial action is acquired along with the business. Liability does not cease with a change of ownership, but it can shift to "deeper pockets."

B. All environmental hazards should be treated seriously and carefully quantified. Sellers, with some justification, tend to argue that many environmental hazards are insignificant because they have lived with them so long without complaints or actual harm to individuals. However, that does not change the fact that harm may occur, and it is compliance with government regulations that is the test. Investors should never give only cursory attention to environmental issues in their enthusiasm to complete a "good deal." It may be "good" because the seller is well aware of the problems.

C. Identification of environmental hazards—estimating their magnitude and recommended remedial action—requires professionals who are knowledgeable in these matters. As with all professionals, there are varying levels of competence, several good solutions, and ample room for differences of opinion. If the condition appears to constitute significant exposure, a second opinion may be warranted. A risk associated with the employment of professions is that they may be required to report the existence of hazards to the appropriate government agency.

QUESTIONS AND PROCEDURES

1. Identify the individual who has the most knowledge of environmental issues within the business. Does this individual have responsibility for monitoring compliance and remedial activities? If not, who does? What is this person's authority and status within the organization?

2. Have there been, or is there now, any EPA or other government environmental agencies, investigations, suits, audits, studies, or charges involving any locations or activities of the business? If yes, summarize and obtain copies of all suits, reports, assessments, complaints, and correspondence. What is their present status?

3. Estimate the cost of all remedial action required to eliminate known environmental hazardous conditions and to comply with government regulations. Estimate the cost of compliance with any scheduled new government regulations.

4. Has the business internally conducted or employed consultants for environmental studies? If yes, obtain copies of the reports. Obtain copies of any phase 1, 2, or 3 studies.

5. Have any environmental activists or media personnel charged this business or the industry in which it operates of having or creating environmental hazards or harming the environment? If yes, obtain full details.

6. Is there a record of or the potential for assets owned by the business to cause significant damage or injury to others, such as pipelines, storage facilities, transmission lines, transportation equipment, etc.? If yes, obtain full details. Quantify the financial exposure and the amount insured.

7. Does this business have any locations where, in the past, it has experienced damage from natural occurring events such as flooding, wind storms, or earthquakes? If yes, what is the probability of reoccurrence, and what protective measures have been taken?

8. Consider separately each parcel of real estate owned or leased by the business. On property where environmental hazards may exist, determine if the hazard is definitely known to exist or suspected, but not certain. Indicate any remedial or preventative steps that have been taken or planned.

9. Do present operations contaminate the soil?

10. Have any past operations of present or former owners or tenants of the real estate contaminated the soil? Who were the prior owners, and what was the use of the real estate?

11. Have any studies involving test borings been conducted? If yes, obtain copies of the reports.

12. Do any neighbors have operations that create environmental hazards that may have migrated onto the business's property?

13. Are there any known toxic waste dumps in the vicinity of the business's property?

14. Are there any underground or surface storage tanks on the business's property? Are any such tanks on neighboring property that may have leaked with material migrating onto the business's property?

15. Are the sewer system and sewage treatment facilities in compliance and adequate?

16. Do any buildings contain asbestos? Is lead-based paint prevalent?

17. Does the business use radioactive material or devices?

18. Are any chemicals used in the business's operations that are considered toxic? If yes, list and describe their use and method of disposal. Where are the dump sites, if any, that are used or have been used?

19. Do any operations of the business release either toxic or nontoxic emissions into the air or water? If yes, list and describe methods of compliance and/or any possible violations.

20. Are there any discharges of waste water on or from the property? Are there any streams or bodies of water on the property or nearby into which wastewater is discharged?

21. Is there any waste oil or coolant used in the operations of the business? If yes, is it stored and disposed of in compliance with all regulations?

22. Are there any PCBs or electrical equipment containing PCBs on the property? Obtain copies of all documents and records relating to the existence or removal of any PCBs.

23. Has any hazardous materials been treated, stored, disposed of, incinerated, or recycled by the business or any of its agents? If yes, describe in detail and the entire "chain of ownership."

24. Except for lubricants or motor oil in insignificant quantities, has any hazardous material ever been spilled, disposed of, discharged, or released on the premises or been transported to other locations for disposal?

25. Has the business been accused of disposing of any waste at a Superfund site?

26. If the property has been utilized for many years, how was waste disposed of prior to the advent of environmental regulations? Was there a pit for burning waste?

27. Are there any environmental hazards that are known or suspected that have not been investigated and remedial action taken because of the cost? Identify any of a magnitude that the financial health of the business could be seriously impacted?

28. Review the record of compliance by organizations employed by the business to dispose of hazardous and/or toxic material.

29. Identify the government agencies responsible for monitoring the business for compliance on environmental matters.

30. Is there current activity in legislative bodies or regulatory agencies that may lead to regulations that could affect the operations of the business? Has any legislation been passed recently that could affect the business? Are there any citizen groups advocating changes in regulations that could affect the business? If yes, obtain full information.

31. Are any remedial projects underway? If yes, identify the total estimated cost, percentage completed, and expenditures to date.

32. What have been the business's expenditures during each of the past three years for remedial or preventative environmental measures? Has the business established any financial reserves to cover environmental cleanup costs, legal fees, and fines? Is there a footnote in the financial statements?

33. What EPA or government permits does the business have? Are there others it should have? Have any applications been rejected or in the process of being rejected? Have any expired or waivers granted?

34. Does the business have an environmental policy manual? If yes, obtain a copy.

35. Request the names and addresses of all regulatory agencies with whom this business has had any direct contact, either through meetings or correspondence. Review the correspondence. Obtain the names and titles of those within the agencies who have been in contact with employees of the business.

36. Who or what firm has advised and/or represented the business on environmental legal issues?

37. What is the amount of fines paid for environmental infractions during the past three years? If any have been paid or assessed but not paid, obtain full information on the cause. Are any fines or regulatory actions being appealed?

38. As a result of concerns over global warming, has management taken or developed plans to reduce carbon dioxide emissions? Could reduction of CO_2 emissions become a major factor in this business's operations?

CHAPTER 30
Debt, Banks, and Financial Institutions

PRIMARY ISSUES AND OBSERVATIONS

A. The identification of all debt and the total amounts owed is the first step, but learning the cost, terms of repayment, and collateral required is equally important. Complete information is essential, and attorneys may be necessary to review the often voluminous and complex documents.

B. The business's ability to obtain credit may be one of its most valuable assets or a liability. The relationship with lenders is worth studying, and with the approval of the business's management, direct solicitations of their opinions could prove invaluable. If an investor expects to retain the indebtedness, early contact is advisable. Relationships between borrowers and lenders often become strained, and the lenders may welcome a new friendly face. The lenders may be worried about losing the credit, or they may look at the investor as their salvation.

C. Lenders normally conduct their own due diligence prior to advancing funds. The interest rates and terms they demand is a direct reflection of their conclusions relative to the overall quality of the business and its management. A lender's primary interest is to profit from interest payments and have the principal returned on schedule. The lender's analysis of future cash flow and associated risk will largely influence the terms required for funding. Collateral functions as a sort of backup insurance become important only when repayment is not achieved. Lenders prefer not to be involved in liquidations and usually make every effort to avoid the process.

QUESTIONS AND PROCEDURES

1. Identify the executive or individuals responsible for screening lenders, approving debt, negotiating debt instruments, and administering debt once incurred. If there is a treasury department, what other services besides debt management does the department provide?

2. List all loans, borrowings, and debt securities outstanding and their basic terms. For each, list the collateral pledged. Review all debt documentation and instruments. Review the interest rate and terms of each for insight into the opinions of lenders as to the quality of the borrower.

3. Conduct a U.C.C. search and compare with the information supplied by the business. Are there records of indebtedness that has been paid off, but for which the liens have not been removed?

4. List each bank that the business has worked with in the past two years. Describe the nature, length of the relationship, and the bank executives responsible for the accounts of the business. Request a list of all bank accounts, the outstanding balances, and the authorized signers on each account. For each bank, determine why it was selected and whether there are any special relationships.

5. List any banks that have declined to grant accounts with the business, made proposals that were rejected, or are presently seeking a relationship with the business.

6. List any investment banks, hedge funds, or individuals who within the past three years have proposed, made, or arranged debt for the business. Describe the nature of the relationship and results with each.

7. Request a list of lines of credit, their cost, limits, and amounts drawn down. Are there covenants that have the practical effect of preventing the lines of credit from being fully drawn down? Do any require compensating balances? Is a lock box system in place, causing all receipts to flow through the bank granting the line of credit?

8. How does the business plan to meet its current and long-term debt obligations? Is there a clearly defined plan? Is the business actively seeking new borrowings, or does it see a need to do so in the near future? Is there an opportunity to refinance at a lower cost? Has or is the business having difficulty in seeking new financing?

9. Is this business in default, or about to default, on any debt obligations? Does this business have systems in place to make loan payments on time?

10. Are any cash investments or securities pledged as collateral?

11. Do any debt obligations give the lender warrants or other rights to acquire equity in the business?

12. What parent company guarantees are outstanding? What is the policy? If the business has subsidiaries or divisions with their own bank accounts,

what level of discretion do they have in selecting banks and administering the accounts?

13. Are there personal guarantees on any of the business's debts?

14. Identify any debt of the business guaranteed by third parties, including credit derivatives. If guarantees exist, identify the guarantor and cost, and the terms of the guarantee.

15. Identify major or any unusual restrictions found in the debt agreements. How aware is management of these covenants, and is there compliance?

16. Is there any off–balance sheet financing? If yes, obtain full information, including the history, guarantees, and present status.

17. Is the value of the collateral pledged relatively consistent with the value of the loans outstanding? Has any effort been made to remove excess collateral?

18. Does the business provide letters of credit? If yes, what is outstanding? Who issues the letters, and how are they backed?

19. Is this business paying competitive interest rates? Is there an opportunity to renegotiate or refinance?

20. How do financial institutions and other lenders view this business and the industry?

21. Is any financing provided by suppliers? If yes, what are the true costs and obligations?

22. Are there any loans from shareholders, directors, or officers? If yes, what are their origin, interest rate, repayment history, and schedule? Are the loans fully documented? Do any of these loans actually constitute delayed compensation?

23. Prepare a list of all leases and their terms. Identify those that are capitalized. What renewal, purchase rights, and other obligations exist? Review the lease documents.

24. Has the business received any tax concessions or loans with covenants to locate to or remain in a specific location?

25. Has all or any segment of the business ever been in or actively considered bankruptcy?

26. Are there any credit rating agencies that have rated the business or any of its debt? If yes, obtain the ratings and evaluate their significance.

CHAPTER 31
Investments, Hedging, and Derivatives

PRIMARY ISSUES AND OBSERVATIONS

A. Investments in this chapter may be broadly defined as any assets that are not immediately used or needed for the operation of the business. Securities, tangible assets, and intangible assets not utilized or needed in the near future should be viewed as investments to be evaluated. The longer a business has been in operation, the greater the probability is that assets exist not essential to the business. The retention or disposal of these assets is a subject of interest for most investors.

Comparing the present book and estimated market value of all investments can be a challenge. The value of marketable securities is simple, but unmarketable securities and all other assets often requires appraisers and others claiming expertise who will voice qualified opinions. Investigators should always be alert to inflated valuations of assets, either in their initial recording or through depreciation manipulation.

B. Hedging and derivatives are a form of investment with their basic purpose to mitigate risk and/or protect assets. Hedging is the technique primarily for protecting against fluctuations in currency and/or commodity values. Hedging protects the assets of the business and allows management to concentrate on the sale unconcerned with factors it cannot control. If the business engages in hedging, there must be an awareness of the risks. The investor must assess the risks, decide if the cost of hedging is justified, and decide if additional risks should be hedged.

C. Derivatives are phenomena that have exploded into prominence since 2000. The term "derivatives" covers a wide array of financial instruments whose returns are linked to or derived from some underlying assets. Their growth has been spectacular but largely unregulated, and their transactions are complex and often not well understood as to the risks involved. Credit default swaps make up the majority of the credit derivatives market. They provide a kind of insurance against nonpayment of corporate debt with the buyer of protection paying an annual premium that is a percentage of the debt covered. Derivatives may be an opportunity for investors willing to accept greater risk in return for superior yields. There exists a variety of derivative instruments that are viewed as exotic and extremely complex. If the business is involved with exotics, extra care in the investigation is warranted.

QUESTIONS AND PROCEDURES

1. Request a list of all cash investments and securities, both marketable and unmarketable. Compare book price to market. Learn the history of each. How have the unmarketable securities been valued, and by whom? Segregate the short-term investments.

2. Identify all loans and investments in default or where a full return or recovery is unlikely.

3. Identify the person or persons responsible for selecting, approving, and monitoring investments? How are the investments made? Identify all investment banks, banks, brokers, or financial advisors utilized.

4. Does the business, or do any shareholders or executives, receive any supplemental benefits by investing through or with any financial institutions? Describe any entertainment or other benefits offered or provided executives by those soliciting the business's investments.

5. Does the business have policies, either formal or informal, governing investments? If written, obtain a copy.

6. Identify all investments in foreign countries and/or currencies.

7. Identify investments most observers would consider high risk, speculative, not presently performing, or ones in which the return, if any, is distant. Are there plans to liquidate any of these investments? Would their liquidation have an insignificant, adverse, or positive influence on the share price of the business?

8. Identify all non-cash investments, such as real estate, minority investments in other businesses, licenses, participation in joint ventures, discontinued businesses, exploration and production contracts, venture

capital investments, etc. Compare the book value to appraisals or other means of estimating probable market value. Identify those the business is considering or actively attempting to sell.

9. Does the business own any assets used in the business that have so appreciated in value that they should be sold?

10. How and where are temporary surplus funds invested?

11. Are there any loans outstanding or loan commitments to shareholders, directors, officers, or employees? If yes, what are their origin, purpose, interest rate, repayment history, and schedule? Are the loans fully documented? Are any of these loans in default?

12. Are there any loans that have been or will be written off in which the business does expect or will not demand repayment? Are written-off loans ever reviewed to learn of the possibility of recovery?

13. Have there been investments made to improperly inflate profits? Have any investment's market value been inflated for financial reporting purposes? Has the business obtained dubious appraisals or avoided independent fair appraisals for fear of the results?

14. Does the business have any pension, profit sharing, or 401(k) plans? Obtain copies of all fund reports, lists of investment audits, and correspondence with government agencies. (See Chapter 20, "Retirement Plans, 401(k)s, and ESOPs," for additional questions.)

15. Are commodities such as energy, grains metals, and feed stocks a significant cost for the business? Can commodity price fluctuations materially affect the profitability of the business? Has this happened? Has protection been sought with futures contracts? Have more exotic techniques such as swaps and options been utilized?

16. Does this business engage in hedging? If yes, against what risks does the business have hedges outstanding? What risks are normally hedged?

17. Has this business ever experienced significant losses through hedging, forward contracts, or other such techniques?

18. Who is responsible for deciding if hedging is advisable and placing the hedges? Does the business have a general attitude or policy towards hedging? What controls are exercised over traders?

19. Identify the financial institutions utilized in obtaining hedge and derivative contracts.

20. During the past three years, has the business experienced significant losses because of a failure to hedge? Have losses been the result of mistaken convictions on the direction of markets?

21. Are there risks associated with this business that are not hedged, but in other businesses are normally hedged?

22. Has this business ever speculated on commodity or currency futures? If yes, obtain full details, including the results.

23. Has the business invested in derivative securities, either in the open market or in private transactions? If yes, identify all outstanding contracts, their purpose, and/or risks from which protection was sought. What are the initial, annual cost and the duration of each contract?

24. Does the business invested in derivatives expect superior yields? Has the business allowed assets to be pledged or loaned to back up derivatives?

25. Who is responsible for evaluating, selecting, and purchasing derivative contracts? Identify the executives that have an actual understanding of derivatives and any potential risks.

26. Has the business recovered credit losses as a result of holding derivative contracts?

27. How does this business reflect derivative expense, gains, or losses on its financial statements?

28. Review how the business records in its financial statements transactions involving hedging and derivatives. Is the recording in accordance with financial standards?

CHAPTER 32
Cash and Cash Management

PRIMARY ISSUES AND OBSERVATIONS

A. An investor must study the composition of the cash account to learn the true amount that is actually available. Studies are compounded by an absence of a universally agreed-upon definition of "cash." Auditors are not in full agreement on their definitions, but most disputes appear to be over what short-term or highly liquid assets may be classified as cash.

B. Individuals managing the cash of the business have a challenge to invest surplus cash yet maintain adequate funds available daily to meet the obligations of the company. Interest is lost forever when cash is sitting in non-interest-bearing accounts. Compounding the problem is that cash receipts are frequently unpredictable.

C. Study all the factors limiting the availability of cash. The cash may be in the business's accounts but restricted from use. The extent of the restrictions, their duration, and origin requires study.

QUESTIONS AND PROCEDURES

1. Who is responsible for management of the cash of the business? Are cash flow projections frequently made, enabling the business to plan its cash requirements to meet its obligations? Obtain copies of internal cash reports and forecasts.

2. How does this business define cash? Identify short-term investments, such as commercial paper and treasury securities, that are recorded as cash.

3. Is the cash restricted in any way by compensating balances, bonding requirements, letters of credit, or other obligations?

4. Is any cash in currencies not readily converted into hard currencies or in blocked accounts?

5. Is a portion of the cash due to "front end," mobilization, or progress payments?

6. Are cash levels highly influenced by seasonal factors?

7. Is there any cash earned outside the United States in foreign accounts that cannot be repatriated without paying taxes? In what currencies is the cash held? What are the business's plans for the use of these funds? How are the funds invested?

8. Are certain levels of cash required by debt covenants, either separately or as a part of current assets?

9. What evidence is there that the business aggressively manages its cash? Does the business know on a daily basis the extent and location of its cash?

10. Does management have a program to avoid losses on foreign exchange? Does the business utilize hedging or derivatives? Have there been significant losses or gains? What is the present exposure? Who is responsible for this risk?

11. Are evaluating customers, granting of credit, and receivable collection major factors in this business? Who is responsible for evaluating credit and making collections? Is the credit approval function closely coordinated with those involved in cash management?

12. Evaluate and describe the credit investigation and approval system and governing policies. To whom does the credit manager report?

13. Does the business factor receivables? If yes, what are the reasons for factoring and who is the factor? What receivables are factored?

14. Is this a business in which employees handle cash on a regular basis? If yes, have there been any incidents of theft or skimming? What controls are in place to control, detect, and deter theft?

15. Does the business buy supplies and materials for cash? Identify any significant purchases made for cash.

16. Does the business print payable checks but hold the checks to conserve cash or until cash is available?

17. What controls exist to prevent improper or unauthorized checks from being issued?

18. Does this business pay its bills promptly? Are vendor payments slow because of cash shortages?

19. Does cash change hands for intracompany transactions?

20. How does the parent company extract cash from the operating subsidiaries or divisions?

21. Does this business have adequate cash combined with borrowing capacity to continue in business for the foreseeable future?

22. What level of cash does management believe is needed to operate the business?

CHAPTER 33
Accounting: General Questions

PRIMARY ISSUES AND OBSERVATIONS

A. A primary objective in studying the financial statements is gaining a satisfactory level of confidence that the statements can be relied upon. This can be accomplished only by in-depth study of all aspects of the accounting systems, the personnel, and the policies. Assuming the financial statements are reliable because they have a clean opinion from their auditors has been the undoing of many investors. Chapter 50, "Outrageous Improprieties," is an incomplete but lengthy list of scandals in corporations, all of which for a period of time enjoyed audits with clean opinions. The record is obvious: a determined unscrupulous management can deceive its auditors.

B. How easily financial reports are understood is a combined measure of the competency of the preparers and the activities of the business. Some businesses have statements that are notoriously difficult to comprehend, such as insurance companies, but most are understood with one reading. Statements with mysterious line items and/or voluminous, often complex footnotes may only reflect the varied activities of an aggressive management, but still require close investigation. Financial statements that are difficult to comprehend are not necessarily an indictment of the business, but they do constitute a warning.

C. While accounting is cloaked in mathematics, never assume that it produces a completely accurate financial picture of the business. Amounts to be placed in reserves, inventory valuations, and overhead allocations are only a few of the areas requiring the recording of reasonable estimates, with all involved aware that they are not precise numbers. In many instances, the issue of "materiality" further complicates matters. Financial statements record history, and there is always a gap between their date of preparation and today. The quality of financial statements depends upon many factors, including the skill of those involved in their preparation, the supporting financial systems, and the objectives of management. An investor must decide if the financials provide an adequate picture of the business's finances.

QUESTIONS AND PROCEDURES

1. In general, how reliable do the financial reports appear to be? Are shareholders, management, and those involved in their preparation willing to warrant to their accuracy?

2. Are the statements audited, reviewed, or compilations?

3. Is the business in full compliance with the Sarbanes-Oxley Act? If not, indicate areas of noncompliance. What changes in the business's policies and procedures were or remain necessary to achieve compliance?

4. Name the public accounting firm engaged for the audit and any fees paid to them during each of the past four years. Identify any other accounting firms used and the fees paid. Obtain approval to review their work papers.

5. Did any of the accounting firms named in Question 4 also prepare tax reports and/or consulting services? If yes, describe in detail the scope of their assignments, the fees paid, and the results.

6. If the opinion of the auditors is qualified in any way, request full information on the reasons for their reservations.

7. Have the auditors been changed in the past five years? If yes, obtain full details.

8. If the business has multiple business units or subsidiaries, do the auditors audit each unit or give only an opinion on the business as a whole?

9. Request copies of any management letters prepared by auditors during the past four years. Identify steps taken, if any, to implement recommendations.

10. Describe any major personnel changes in the financial departments within the past two years and reasons for the changes.

11. Describe any financial systems undergoing major revisions and the reasons why they are changing. Are systems that have been introduced within the past two years functioning as planned?

12. Are there any significant differences between financial statements, tax returns, and SEC filings? If yes, determine the reasons.

13. If there are multiple divisions or subsidiaries, are accounting policies uniform and formats identical? Do all use the same chart of accounts? If not, describe reasons for differences.

14. Are the financial statements for the past five years in essentially the same format so trends and ratios may be calculated? Are they in sufficient detail to determine trends in expense categories?

15. Does the business have internal auditors? Review copies of their reports. What is the scope of their authority and role? Do they audit nonfinancial matters? To whom do they report? Obtain copies of their reports.

16. Are any accounting functions other than auditing contracted out? Have any departments or functions been outsourced?

17. How many days after the close of a month are financial statements produced? How many weeks after the close of the fiscal year are financial reports complete?

18. Is the business rigid in closing each accounting period as scheduled? Is there any evidence of accounting periods being held open to improve results?

19. Describe the business's overall systems of internal controls. Are they adequate, or are they undergoing improvement? Are the controls well established, monitored, and enforced? Have the auditors expressed an opinion on this subject? Has the audit committee of the board of directors reviewed and voiced an opinion?

20. What controls, if any, exist to monitor and approve expenses of senior management?

21. Has the quality of the financial statements been influenced by internal pressures to achieve budgeted targets, management incentive plans, or corporate goals?

22. Are the line items on the financial statements and any accompanying notes clear and understandable? (If any are not, gaining full knowledge and comprehension is essential to understanding the reports.)

23. Obtain or construct an organization chart of the financial operations, showing both personnel and functions.

24. Has the business ever found it necessary to restate earnings? If yes, obtain full details.

25. What is this business's overall philosophy and attitude towards accounting? What is the status of the CFO? Is there emphasis on obtaining accurate and timely reports? Is there pressure to increase or withhold earnings?

CHAPTER 34
Accounting Policies

PRIMARY ISSUES AND OBSERVATIONS

A. A complete understanding of a business's financial condition is impossible without knowledge of the underlying policies. With understanding comes confidence, or a lack of confidence, that one can rely upon the statements. If a lack of confidence develops that cannot be quickly resolved, the investor will be wise to seek other places for his money. If an investor discovers a serious problem within the financial statements, he can assume the probability is high that he has not discovered them all.

B. Accounting policies, proper and improper, can be used to affect the results and further management's objectives. During the study, an investigator should attempt to learn either from candid comments of employees or by perception to ascertain the influence of management's objectives. Do accounting personnel believe they have a mandate to maximize or reduce earnings with accounting treatment?

C. Regardless of how charming, prominent, and successful the major shareholder or CEO of the seller is, investigators should always assume there is a chance that outward appearances are a deception. All of the businesses mentioned in Chapter 50, "Outrageous Improprieties," were managed by executives whom no one suspected, and they did not act alone. The identification of improper, unorthodox accounting policies or those contrary to common practices constitutes a primary due diligence objective. The detailed study of the financial statements and how they were created is the best hope of ferreting out improper and usually illegal activities.

QUESTIONS AND PROCEDURES

1. Are the annual financial statements prepared in accordance with GAAP and AICPA? If not, identify deviations.
2. Is the business in full compliance with the Sarbanes-Oxley Act? If not, where is it not in compliance? What changes in the business's operations were or are necessary to fully comply with the act?
3. Obtain a chart of accounts and any manuals of accounting policy.
4. Describe accounting principles, policies, and actual practices employed in each of the categories listed. Also:

   - Identify any utilized to intentionally increase or delay income recognition.
   - Identify any policies that deviate from those of the investor.
   - Identify policies that are written and those unwritten.
   - Identify polices that are not followed in practice.
   - Identify policies interpreted and skewed to further management objectives.
   - Identify policies that have had a significant impact upon reported earnings, including:

     a) Inventory (see Chapter 37)
     b) Percentage of completion
     c) Reserves and allowances
     d) Capitalization vs. expensing
     e) Prepayments
     f) Payables
     g) Inclusion or exclusion of subsidiaries or affiliates in consolidated returns
     h) Revenue and income matching and/or recognition
     i) Cost accounting and overhead allocation
     j) Retirement plan and stock option expenses
     k) Depreciation
     l) Intracompany transactions (see Chapter 43)
     m) Receivables, timing and recognition (see Chapter 35)
     n) Off–balance sheet entities, liabilities, assets or investments
     o) Discontinued operations and businesses
     p) Anticipated expense accruals
     q) Expense of stock options

5. Identify all of the above policies that have a material impact upon income.

6. What differences in results would have occurred if the accounting policies of the investor had been applied?

7. Describe the year-to-year consistency of application of accounting policies, principles, and procedures. Identify any changes in the past five years and their causes. Have any of the changes been controversial?

8. Do any subsidiaries, joint ventures, affiliates, or companies in which the business has a significant investment have different fiscal years?

9. Does the business use accounting policies to deliberately increase reported income or to hold back or reduce income? If yes, identify the policies and all those involved in carrying out the policies. Are these policies known to other employees, shareholders, and investors?

10. Have any of the accounting policies been challenged by the auditors, government agencies, or investors? If yes, obtain complete details.

11. Does the business have any pending requests to change accounting policies and practices? Are there any changes the business may be compelled to make?

12. Has the business been engaged in any programs that could be considered restructuring? If yes, what has been the accounting policies and approach?

13. How has the business accounted for any acquisitions within the past three years?

14. Has this business changed its fiscal year within the last five years? If yes, what were the reasons?

15. Have any asset values been increased and depreciation schedules manipulated to affect taxes and income?

16. Have reserves been established to cover the cost of liquidating discontinued operations? How are the reserves established, and will they materially affect future reported income?

17. Is there any indication of premature recognition of litigation settlements, claims, tax settlements, or other similar unresolved issues?

18. If percentage of completion accounting is utilized, answer the following questions:

- Are original job cost estimates reasonably accurate? What is the overall competency of the estimators?

- What is the method of determining the percentage completed of work in progress? Who makes the estimates?

- What is the formula for recording income or losses on work in progress? Is it a direct percentage to total job cost, or does it vary?

- Is there any indication that percentage of completion accounting has been manipulated to either enhance or delay income?
- Compare the amount of profit or loss remaining upon completion of jobs with estimates made upon receipt of the orders.

CHAPTER 35
Accounts and Notes Receivable

PRIMARY ISSUES AND OBSERVATIONS

A. The ability to collect receivables on a timely basis and assess their validity is a primary concern. A precise estimate of both the percentage of total receivables that will become cash and the timing of such receipts is a priority concern for investors. A study of the history of receivable collections and the current account may provide confidence that all or nearly all will be collected. Study may also reveal that many will either be collected only with great difficulty, or not at all. The actual value of the receivables is often a contentious issue in an investor's negotiations. It is not unusual for an investor after the due diligence study to know more about the account than the senior management of the seller.

The receivable account is a current asset, and its content directly affects both the net worth and income of the business. Managements wishing to manipulate reported income have found the receivable account a ready target, using both crude and ingenious methods. Adding fictitious receivables, not writing off the uncollectible, and premature billings all increase income. Income can be delayed to a later time by creating unjustified large reserves for bad debts and/or deliberate slow invoices to customers. Investigators should be alert for any impropriety.

B. Receivables are the best opportunity to identify the actual customers of the business and the revenues that individual customers and/or types of customers generate. Receivables are the acid test of who the customers are and what products or services are being sold.

Receivables will clearly demonstrate what is being sold today, but they should not be viewed as an omen as to what may be sold in the future.

C. Displeased customers either are slow to pay or refuse to pay invoices. As a consequence, a review of contested receivables will quickly reveal problems the business is experiencing. How serious the problems are, their magnitude, and what remedial steps, if any, management has taken should be evaluated.

QUESTIONS AND PROCEDURES

1. Request any internal reports summarizing receivables by amount and age. If none are available, prepare such a report.

2. How does the business define "current" and "past due" receivables, both from a reporting and practical basis? Prepare a list of customers past due and identify the causes, if possible.

3. Once a receivable is considered past due, what steps are taken to collect, and who is responsible for collections? Who makes the final decision to commence aggressive measures to collect? Who decides when a receivable is uncollectible and should be written off?

4. How well are receivable collections coordinated with sales and credit personnel? Do they assist in collection of problem receivables? Who negotiates with customers relative to problem receivables? Who places customers on a COD basis?

5. How are discounts, returns, rebates, claims either by or against customers, change orders, installment sales, and consignment sales recorded, and the receivable account affected?

6. Identify customer contracts covering projects or services completed that remain open with the final billing yet to be settled. Identify disputed receivables. Learn the circumstances and the status of negotiations, and estimate the probable outcome.

7. Identify the major customer receivables. What percentage of the business does each customer represent? Are any a problem either by disputes or slow payment? If possible, locate a receivable report from a prior period (the prior year, if available) to learn of differences, if any, in the customers.

8. Are there any receivables outstanding from customers known to have financial problems? Are these customers on a COD basis?

9. Identify customers who are notoriously slow to pay but eventually do. Are any permitted delayed payment as a technique to provide customer financing and as an inducement to make the sale?

10. Describe any reserves for doubtful or uncollectible accounts and how they are determined. Does the business have a history of establishing

adequate reserves? Does the business reserve excess amounts, or write off accounts prematurely, to delay taxes? Compare actual losses with reserves for the past two fiscal years.

11. Describe any collateralized accounts or notes receivable.

12. Describe any pledging, factoring, or other restrictions. If factoring or receivables occurs, determine the reason, cost, procedures, and financial institution used.

13. Describe the accounting for retentions. If appropriate, include in the accounts receivable ageing or make a separate report. Indicate when and how much of the retainage is likely to be collected. Are any of the jobs in trouble for which there is retainage?

14. Describe the amount and quality of non-trade receivables, such as those arising from royalties or sale of assets.

15. Request a list of all receivables and/or notes due from shareholders, businesses controlled by shareholders, directors, or management.

16. How are intercompany sales between divisions and subsidiaries recorded and processed? Do receivables result?

17. List all notes receivable, debtor, interest rate, retirement schedule, collateral, liens, whether payments are up to date, probability of collection, and the origin of the note.

18. If the business uses percentage of completion accounting, determine the methods, accuracy, and validity of the "unbilled receivable." Give attention to the procedure for income recognition during jobs in progress, and compare closed jobs with past income recognition. (See Chapter 34)

19. Identify customers who pay very slowly but eventually do pay. What is their motivation?

20. Does the business use collection agencies? If yes, when are receivables referred, and what are the costs? What was the volume of receivables referred to collection agencies in the past year and the amounts recovered?

21. What has been the business's record of eventually recovering written off bad debts? Is this a hidden asset? Is there foreclosed collateral that may have value?

22. Have invoices been backdated to accelerate income? Are some months "held open" to include shipments or services performed after the months end? Are some customers billed prematurely to enhance reported income?

23. If sales are made with the customer having the right to return any unsold merchandise, how is this recorded? Is marked-down or returned merchandise a major factor in this business?

CHAPTER 36
Taxes

PRIMARY ISSUES AND OBSERVATIONS

A. Taxes are another cost of business. As with all costs, it is management's responsibility to plan and control the expense. How well this is accomplished is a primary subject for inquiry. Management's policies and attitude towards taxes is a factor to evaluate, as answers to the list of questions are pursued. Management may accept taxes as a normal cost of business to be carefully scrutinized but assigned to professionals with their conclusions accepted. Other managements pursue an aggressive policy to pay minimal taxes through use of tax shelters, foreign accounts, transfer pricing, "gray area" accounting, or other techniques to avoid or reduce taxes. For most businesses, the policies and practices are somewhere in between these two extremes. Understanding how the business administers and processes taxes is a major factor for study.

B. An investor should identify all tax obligations and evaluate their impact upon the business. Give particular attention to taxes that provide either competitive advantages or noncompetitive disadvantages. If there are serious noncompetitive disadvantages, the next issue becomes one of identifying possible remedies.

C. The frequency and magnitude of controversies, tax disputes, and litigation is an indication of both the business's attitude towards payment of taxes and the opinion of the taxing bodies towards the business. Ample anecdotal evidence indicates once a business and/or its tax professionals acquire a reputation for aggressive and combative tax policies, there is a reaction. The reaction can be in the form of increased and closer scrutiny of returns, more aggressive and frequent audits, refusal to compromise, and willingness to litigate.

A business may find the cost of an overly combative attitude towards taxes greater than the possible savings. But keep in mind, professionals bill by the hour.

QUESTIONS AND PROCEDURES

1. Who in the business is responsible for preparing tax reports, compliance, protests, and authorizing payments? Identify auditors, tax consultants, attorneys, or other nonemployees providing assistance, their roles, and the amounts paid to each during the past two years.

2. List all governments and government agencies—federal, state, local, and foreign—to which tax reports must be filed and/or taxes paid. Obtain copies for the past three years.

3. Request for each of the taxing bodies the following information: any amounts owed but not paid, any amounts in dispute, and any reports not filed on time.

4. Are there any outstanding tax controversies in which unfavorable rulings could result in penalties, fines, and/or criminal charges? Are there controversies that could result in favorable rulings materially benefiting the business? If yes, obtain full information, including present status and time of anticipated resolution. Are these reflected on the balance sheet?

5. Identify tax positions taken by the business that are likely to be challenged by auditors or tax authorities. What are the consequences if the challenges prevail?

6. Identify any reserves established for tax purposes. For each reserve, determine the amount, the basis for existence, and the probability of being successfully challenged by auditors and/or tax authorities.

7. When was the last U.S. Internal Revenue Service (IRS) audit, and what was the result? What years are still open?

8. Identify any IRS, state, local, or foreign tax audits in progress, scheduled, or expected within the next six months. Is there any reason for concern about the outcome of the audits?

9. Identify any tax refunds agreed upon but not yet received. Identify any applications for tax refunds that are outstanding. How are anticipated tax refunds reflected in the financial statements?

10. Identify any current or potential disputes with any taxing bodies that are or may result in litigation. Segregate those in which the business is asked to pay additional funds from those in which the business is requesting a refund. For each, obtain full information.

11. Has there been a need, and has management made any provisions, for claims, renegotiation, revisions, or loss of determinations? If yes, how are they reflected in the financial statements?

12. Compare the actual or effective tax rate with the statutory rate. Determine the reasons for the differences.

13. Describe the circumstances and procedures that give rise to deferred taxes. Under what conditions would deferred taxes become due and payable?

14. Identify all tax loss carry forwards (NOLs) and/or tax credits and the year of their expiration. What was their origin?

15. Has the business received any tax concessions as a result of locating to a particular location? If yes, describe the circumstances, terms, and obligations of the business.

16. Is tax planning a major consideration in how international business is conducted? Is tax planning a factor in intercompany sales, loans, and other internal transactions? Does the business engage in transfer pricing? Has the business been suspected or accused of transfer pricing practices?

17. Was the business's place of incorporation or location influenced or determined for tax advantages? Does the business have banking or shell subsidiaries in tax havens? If yes, obtain full information.

18. Are any changes being proposed in the tax codes at any level of government that would have either a beneficial or a serious adverse effect upon the business?

19. Has the business requested or received any private letter tax rulings from the IRS? It yes, obtain copies. Have any requests for rulings been rejected?

20. How does this business's state and local taxes compare with competitors? Are state and local tax rates a factor in attracting or retaining employees?

21. Review the tax status and obligations of all foreign subsidiaries, both active and inactive. Were any established for tax purposes rather than for business operations?

22. What are the owners or major shareholder's tax basis of their investments in the business? Estimate their percentage gain if the business is sold. In the event of an asset sale, would depreciation recapture be a significant problem?

23. Have asset values ever been inflated or reduced to affect taxes?

24. Has this business utilized tax shelters? If yes, obtain full information, including their origin and savings realized. Are any being challenged by taxing entities?

25. Has the business ever sought political assistance in resolving tax matters? If yes, what happened?

26. Have payroll taxes been withheld and promptly remitted to the government?

CHAPTER 37
Inventory

PRIMARY ISSUES AND OBSERVATIONS

A. Inventory valuation involves subjective policy decisions that can result in usable approximations of total value, but the value will never be precise. An accurate count is only the first step in determining value. How management classifies inventory into the categories of current, slow moving, obsolete, or scrap is a very subjective and sometimes controversial exercise. Delaying or accelerating write-offs and downs directly affects reported income. Final pricing of the inventory involving overhead allocations and accounting policies may have the greatest impact of all upon the total value. All of these activities constitute opportunities for error and/or manipulation of value.

B. Inventory studies should be in depth, comprehensive, and with all aspects of the inventory studied. Inventory valuation has always been a tempting opportunity for management to increase or decrease earnings. Some of management's policies may have had only minor or insignificant effects, but others constitute fraud. An investor can achieve confidence in the inventory value only after a study of the composition and methods of valuation. An investor's investigators are advised to physically inspect the inventory, select representative samples, and then review how each is recorded and valued in the business's material control and financial records.

C. During an investor's study of the inventory, management policies and practices will become apparent regardless of any prior claims. The emphasis may be on operational requirements with an adequate and correct inventory to meet production and customer requirements. Others may be more concerned with valuation and financial reporting, and many will be a combination of both. An investor, by learning management's attitude towards inventory, will likely find the same attitude prevails in all other aspects of the business.

QUESTIONS AND PROCEDURES

1. Determine the book value of inventory by location and by product line. For each product line, calculate the number of annual turns. Define inventory broadly to include all elements in Question 2 below.

2. Determine by product line the composition of the inventory, the dollar amount, and the percentage of the total inventory each category below represents:

    a) Raw materials

    b) Components or parts manufactured in house

    c) Components or parts purchased

    d) Work in progress

    e) Finished goods

    f) Labor and overhead

    g) Consigned material or parts

    h) Tools and supplies (not expensed)

3. During the past 12 months, what was the inventory's high and low points for each product line, and in which month did the highs and lows occur?

4. Determine the causes for any significant increases or decreases in inventory levels during the past 12 months. Evaluate the importance of seasonal factors.

5. Does management have a program to reduce inventory levels? Has management determined how low inventory levels may be reduced before adversely affecting deliveries and sales? Does management have a "just in time" program for receiving purchased parts and components?

6. Is inventory cost recorded on a LIFO or FIFO basis? If recorded on a LIFO basis, what is the amount of the reserve created? Does management have any plans to change the cost method?

7. How is "market value" determined and applied in valuing inventory at "cost or market," whichever is lower?

8. How often are physical inventories taken? When was the last inventory taken, and when is the next one scheduled? Do auditors observe inventories? Are spot checks and sample counts taken during the fiscal year? Are inventories counted in their entirety, or are random or representative samples counted? Are statistical techniques used in inventory counts?

9. What were the amounts of year-end inventory adjustments by location or product line for the past two years? If the adjustments were significant, what were the causes?

10. Have inventory reserves been recorded on the financial statements? How were they calculated? Does past history justify the level of reserves?

11. What is management's definition and policy to classify inventory as excess or slow moving? Is it written down in value? What is the amount by product line?

12. What is management's definition and policy to classify inventory as obsolete or scrap? How is it recorded? How is obsolete inventory disposed of, sold, or junked? Does a quantity of obsolete inventory remain to be discarded?

13. What percentage or other methods are used to calculate the overhead costs applied to inventory works in progress or finished products? Is there any evidence of excessive overhead charges concealed in inventory?

14. Is there a deviation in actual practice from the formal policies relative to definitions, pricing, and disposition of obsolete, excess, and slow-moving inventory?

15. Is inventory readily identified, orderly stored, and easily located, with locations well marked? Does any appear soiled or dust covered?

16. In the event of an orderly liquidation of the inventory, what is estimated to be the net realizable value?

17. Has inventory been aggressively written down or relocated to reduce or delay taxes?

18. What evidence is there that all or portions of the inventory are undervalued? Have commodity prices had a significant impact on value?

19. Is any inventory not owned by the business kept on a consignment basis? If yes, is it segregated and easily identified?

20. Does the business have inventory out on a consignment basis? If yes, how is this counted and recorded?

21. Does the business store sold products until the customers request delivery? Are these products segregated? Are customers charged storage fees?

22. What happens to excess material or parts charged to particular jobs or works in progress that are not used? What happens to defective products?

23. Has management made changes in its material or inventory control systems within the past two years and are any contemplated? If yes, determine reasons and outcome. Is management generally satisfied with the present systems? How accurate do the records appear?

24. Has there been inventory losses due to theft or other mysterious disappearances? Is physical security a major concern in protecting the inventory?

25. Does the business have the right to return inventory to vendors? If yes, what are the amounts permissible and the normal restocking charges? Does management return excess inventory?

26. Do dealers, distributors, or customers have the right to return merchandise? What is the value of merchandise returned during the past year? How are returned goods valued and recorded?

27. Is the inventory balanced? Determine or estimate the percentage of inventory that turns very slowly compared to the remainder.

28. Is any material amount of inventory in transit between business units of the business? If yes, how is it tracked and recorded?

29. How are scrap sales recorded?

30. Has any event occurred or been observed in which inventory was intentionally or inadvertently counted or recorded incorrectly?

31. Overall, does management consider the present inventory to be excessive, too low, or within a reasonable range?

32. Are any competitors known to have an advantage or disadvantage because of their inventory levels or locations?

33. Is inventory purchased and/or built for firm orders or in anticipation of orders? If in anticipation, how accurate have been sales forecasts?

34. Is inventory bar coded?

35. Is the inventory pledged as collateral?

CHAPTER 38
Fixed and Other Assets

PRIMARY ISSUES AND OBSERVATIONS

A. The due diligence challenge is to determine exactly what the tangible assets of the business are, how accurately they are recorded, and their value. The larger the business, the greater the chances are that not all assets are reflected in the financial statements. The longer a business has been around increases the probability of unrecorded assets and of their book values having little correlation with present market values. Compounding the problems is that for many accounting departments, maintaining up-to-date asset records is a not a pressing priority. Sellers often point with considerable justification that depreciated book values are well below actual market value or replacement cost in an effort to justify their price expectations. The buyer needs to be sufficiently knowledgeable about the assets to evaluate the arguments.

B. Intangible assets are usually easy to identify, but their value, if any, may be more complicated. Their origin and how their original value was determined is a good place to start. Most investors and managements find intangible assets on a balance sheet undesirable, and often seek to implement a means for their elimination. Amortization over a period of time or total write-offs will not affect cash flow, but both affect reported income and book value per share. If the investor acquires the intangible assets, he will have to decide their future based on his overall strategy.

Another category of intangible assets may have great value, but they do not appear on the balance sheet. They include the name of the business, names under which it conducts business, its reputation with all parties, its established relationships, and the assembled workforce. These are the assets a business accumulated since its inception that would be extremely costly, if not impossible, to replace.

C. "Other Assets" may be a separate line item that is partly a mystery account and catchall for assets not readily classified. Most are not essential to the continued operation of the business. "Discontinued businesses" and "Assets held for sale" are commonly found in this account, if not appearing in separate accounts. The account may contain assets that are exclusively used by executives, the remains of failed ventures, or assets acquired by discredited former executives. Investors should request a list of every asset in the account, large and small, as they may discover some surprises. The existence and origin of the assets may provide more important insight into the seller's history and management's activities than the actual value of the assets.

QUESTIONS AND PROCEDURES

1. Review each category of fixed assets as they appear on the balance sheet and obtain a description of the major assets in each category, their age, cost, and depreciated value. Identify assets located in other countries.

2. Does the business have clear policies regarding the assets to be capitalized and those expensed? Is there any evidence of the policy not being followed? Identify any expenses that have been capitalized.

3. How accurate and complete are the business's fixed asset records? When was an actual inventory of the fixed assets last taken? Do the assets have an identifying number attached?

4. What is the estimated market value of tangible assets that are fully depreciated or not listed in financial records?

5. Compare annual depreciation expense with capital expenditures and maintenance and repair expenses for the assets. What does this comparison portend for future cash flow and cash requirements? Obtain or develop a forecast of capital expenditures for the next three years.

6. What are the depreciation and amortization policies used? Have they been consistently applied during the past five years? Are they the same for book and tax purposes? Identify assets for which the book value differs from the tax value.

7. For each category of assets, how does the depreciated book value compare to estimated market value? Identify individual major assets that have a material difference between book and market value. Do leasehold improvements have any market value?

8. Identify any assets that have been either written up or written down on financial reports during the past two years. If there are any, determine the reasons.

9. Have there been any formal or informal appraisals of assets? If yes, obtain copies and/or a summary of the results.

10. Identify any assets with substantial market value that could be sold without materially affecting the business.

11. Identify any assets used in the business with substantial market value that are not producing an adequate return on the investment and could be sold.

12. Does management consider maintenance and repair costs a significant expense? What were they last year? Do they indicate some assets should be replaced? Are these costs excessive by industry standards?

13. Identify and describe any fixed assets that were constructed by employees or purchased from affiliated businesses? What was the method of determining their cost and recording their value on the financial statements?

14. Request a list of all intangible assets and their value represented on the balance sheet. What was the origin and original valuation of each intangible asset? What amortization schedule is used? Do any of these assets have value beyond their original purpose? Do any have a market value and could be sold?

15. Are there valuable intangible assets and intellectual property not protected by copyrights or patents? Are any of these assets being challenged? Has the proprietary rights to any been diminished or lost by management decisions or neglecting to assert defenses?

16. What prepayments are reported as assets? Obtain a complete list. Is the present amount a normal level?

17. If the balance sheet has a category or line item of "Other Assets," list and describe each asset and its valuation basis.

18. Describe any unconsolidated subsidiaries or joint ventures, their estimated value, and income or losses from each. At what value, and where, are investments in these assets recorded in the financial statements? Compare book value to probable market value.

19. Describe any minority investments in other businesses, their purpose, book value, market value, and history.

20. Is management aware of any unrecorded assets, such as written-off receivables, options, notes, assets received for defaulted receivables, and patents or licenses?

21. Request a list of all vehicles, including trucks and trailers owned or leased. Determine their make and age. What is the business's policy on type of automobiles and employee use of automobiles? Who are assigned automobiles?

22. Request a list of aircraft owned or leased. Estimate their market value. What is the use of the aircraft and who flies in them?

23. Request a list of watercraft owned or leased and determine their use.

24. Request a list of hunting, fishing, or other recreational facilities owned or leased. For each, determine their use. Are any primarily for the use of senior executives?

25. Identify all assets of significance essentially unrelated to the business's operations, such as artwork and those acquired as a result of hobbies, interests, or whims of past or present shareholders or executives.

26. Does the business own or lease any houses, apartments, or condominiums? If yes, determine their use and purpose.

27. Does the business have segregated assets "Held for Sale" or classified as discontinued? If yes, list and describe the circumstances and the associated values. What is the status of the effort to sell the assets and the probable amounts to be realized?

28. Does the business have security programs to protect its assets and employees? Who is responsible? What has been the history of losses from theft, vandalism, terrorism, and natural disasters? Is security a major concern and potential problem area?

29. Does the business utilize or store any assets it does not own or lease?

30. Develop a separate list of all assets utilized in the business that are not owned but leased. Conduct a search for such leased assets.

31. If the business has reserves of natural resources, how are they estimated and valued? Obtain copies of geological reports and value estimates. Is there any evidence that the reserves are under- or overvalued, or that the values are highly controversial? Has the compensation of any employees been affected or tied to the level of reserves?

CHAPTER 39
Liabilities

PRIMARY ISSUES AND OBSERVATIONS

A. A study of liabilities involves identifying and understanding all liabilities reflected on the balance sheet plus a search for those not recorded. It is unlikely that the exact sum of liabilities on any given date will ever become known, nor is precision necessary. The investor's general objective should be one of gaining confidence that all liabilities are identified, understood, and that there will be no unpleasant future surprises. For any business in operation, there are a large number of liabilities not appearing on its balance sheet. Most are essential to the business's operations, such as those incurred after the date of the balance sheet and the outstanding purchase commitments. Investors will be concerned and will worry about the unrecorded liabilities and who will be responsible if the business is acquired.

B. In addition to verifying the amount of a liability, the timing of when an obligation must be paid or should have been paid must be determined. A debt due to be repaid next week is a very different note from one that can be paid next year or easily refinanced. Investors will be wise to construct a schedule of when payments are due on both an individual and consolidated basis.

C. During the study of liabilities, an investigator should look for any evidence of accelerated or delayed recognition of liabilities to affect the income statement. The liability account for payables may be most revealing. Recording liabilities promptly and accurately is the first step, and the second is cutting and releasing the check to the creditor. Both steps should be reviewed.

QUESTIONS AND PROCEDURES

1. For each balance sheet liability line item, determine their actual composition and the amount in the various categories. Compare with the chart of accounts. (See Chapter 30,"Debt, Banks, and Financial Institutions," for detailed questions on debt and debt instruments.)

2. Conduct a search for all unrecorded liabilities not reflected in the financial statements. The search should include all possible liabilities including, but not limited to, the following: (Do not assume this is a complete list; see Chapter 46, "Off–Balance Sheet Items," for further details.)

   a) Participation in partnerships

   b) Deferred compensation

   c) Letters of credit

   d) Guarantees of all types

   e) Outstanding purchase orders or contracts

   f) Severance pay commitments

   g) Stock repurchases obligations

   h) Stock option cost

   i) Litigation settlements

   j) Environmental remedial expenses

   k) Retirement plan funding

3. Classify accounts payable by age. What is the business's policy on paying payables? Are discounts taken? Are invoices paid on a timely basis? Is the availability of cash a factor in deciding when to pay invoices? Are some vendors given preference as to when they are paid?

4. Identify any invoices in which payment is withheld because of disputes with the vendor. Determine the nature of the disputes and estimate the probable outcome.

5. Is this business on a COD basis with any vendors?

6. If there are accrued liabilities, how were these calculated, and are they adequate? Are there other liabilities that should have been accrued but were not?

7. Are the systems and procedures such that liabilities are promptly recorded and the last balance sheet accurately reflects the liabilities as of that date? Is there any evidence that invoices are not promptly processed and recorded?

8. If there are "advances on contracts," "billings in excess of costs and estimated earnings," or similar accounts, determine how these entries arose,

how they were calculated, and how they were relieved. Evaluate the systems and accuracy of the account.

9. If there are minority interests held by others in subsidiaries, partnerships, joint ventures, or other business structures, how are these valued and what is their history?

10. Does this business record vacation and/or sick leave benefits as a liability?

11. Have all monies withheld by the business from employees or collected from customers for income taxes, social security, unemployment insurance, and sales, excise, and use taxes been collected or withheld, and either paid to the respective government agencies or set aside in accounts for such purpose? Has the business ever been accused of not properly withholding or remitting such funds?

12. Are liabilities recorded for underfunding of any benefit plans? Are there liabilities that should be recorded? If such liabilities exist, review how they were calculated.

13. Is there a liability account established to offset income reported on an incomplete installment sale?

14. If the business is involved in arranging customer financing, do the financing institutions have recourse to the business in the event of customer defaults?

15. Are there any large contracts or commitments not in the ordinary course of business requiring future payments?

16. If the business has made any acquisitions in the past seven years, are there any contingency obligations to the sellers based on the performance of the acquired business or other events? If yes, obtain complete information. Are there any disputes over the amount of payment?

17. Does the business have buy-sell agreements with shareholders requiring the business to repurchase shares in the event of the shareholder's termination or other triggering events?

18. Are there any obligations of the business to repurchase shares or assist financially option holders when they exercise their options?

CHAPTER 40

Cost of Sales and Gross Profit

PRIMARY ISSUES AND OBSERVATIONS

A. Cost of sales and gross profit percentages and trends are invaluable statistics for management and in the study of a business. However, their underlying composition must be known and understood. Cost of sales consists of material, labor, and overhead, but each requires careful definition. Gross profit is normally the profit before selling and administrative expenses. In well-managed businesses, the cost of sales and gross profit levels are closely monitored, accompanied by constant pressure and programs for improvement. (Gross profit is also referred to as "gross margin." "Income from operations" is the income reported prior to discontinued operations, interest, taxes, etc.)

B. Comparisons of cost of sale and gross profit percentages with other similar industries or competitors can be misleading because of lack of uniformity between businesses as to the expenses assigned to cost of sales. The most common cost of sales percentage is the ratio of cost of sales to revenues, but both pricing and volume changes will affect the actual cost of sales percentages.

C. If businesses have multiple business units, the cost of sale total in consolidated financial reports is of limited value, and each business unit's cost must be reviewed separately. Wide variations in cost of sales percentages for business units may be concealed in the total. The causes and remedies for product or service lines with low gross profits should be a priority area of study.

QUESTIONS AND PROCEDURES

1. Determine the composition of the cost of sales accounts, paying particular attention to the overhead accounts and the allocation of shared expenses.

2. Have there been any changes in the composition of the cost of sales accounts during the past three years? Have there been any significant cost increases in labor or material not passed on to customers?

3. Calculate by product line the ratio of cost of sales to revenues for the past three years, and then determine the reasons for any changes in the percentages. Are any trends apparent?

4. If possible, calculate the cost per unit of production, such as barrels, cases, and tons or similar manufactured products. What are the trends?

5. Is the gross profit and percentage of gross profit for each product line or profit center increasing, decreasing, or remaining constant? Determine the causes. Rank the product lines by their percentage of gross profit.

6. Determine for the past year the dollar amount of material, labor, and overhead in cost of sales for each product line or business unit. Are the percentages of any of these changing? If so, determine the causes.

7. What are the principle elements of cost included in overhead, and their method of calculation and allocation? Are the amounts allocated considered fair, or a source of internal controversy?

8. Are there active programs in place to reduce the cost of sales? Are there established objectives?

9. What cost accounting systems are used to calculate components of cost of sales for each product line? If significant variances result, evaluate causes.

10. Is the gross profit percentage relatively similar month after month? If not, investigate the causes.

11. Is the percentage of gross profit significantly higher or lower than the industry average?

12. Evaluate the impact of increases or decreases in volume of sales and production levels on the cost of sales. What is considered the optimum level of production to achieve the lowest cost of sales?

13. Are increases or decreases in cost of sales readily reflected in prices?

14. Has the business established target goals for gross profits and margins? Is there a gross profit percentage considered unacceptable that triggers divestment or liquidation discussions and decisions?

CHAPTER 41
Selling and General and Administrative Expenses (SG&A)

PRIMARY ISSUES AND OBSERVATIONS

A. Selling and administrative expenses are commonly lumped together into one summary account, but a study of the business requires learning the nature of the individual components. In the study, investigators should seek to discover all expenses that can or should be eliminated in the event of a change in control. Every dollar of expense is one less dollar of pretax profit.

B. Selling expense components cannot be readily compared to those of other businesses unless there is certainty that similar expenses are being compared. Selling expense levels should be equated with the revenues and gross profits that result. A high or low percentage of selling expense is not necessarily bad or good. Selling expenses reflect the methods of selling a business elects to use, and only the results will demonstrate the wisdom of the choice. A successful business may use exclusively direct salesmen who are employees, while an equally successful competitor may sell through outside representatives or commission agents.

C. Administrative expenses include, but are not limited to, all the expenses associated with management of the business. These expenses should be evaluated for reasonableness and searched for improprieties or perquisites not previously disclosed. In this category of expense are found the true costs of the CEO and other executives. Their expenses may be concealed or mixed with other accounts, but they should be somewhere in the administrative accounts.

QUESTIONS AND PROCEDURES

1. Determine the composition of selling expenses and the amount in each for the past two years. How are the costs of information technology systems, including the Internet, classified?

2. Determine the composition of the administrative accounts and the amount in each for the past two years. Identify any selling expenses listed in Question 3 below that are classified as administrative expenses.

3. Determine elements of selling that are included as selling expense, advertising, marketing support, estimating, order processing, customer support, representative or dealers' expense, salaries, and/or incentives for sales personnel facility expense and any other expenses considered selling expenses.

4. What were the selling expenses for each product line and their percentage of total revenues for the product line or business unit? Is the dollar amount and percentage increasing, decreasing, or remaining relatively constant? If there are changes, what are the causes?

5. Are any selling expenses shared or allocated? If yes, review the method of allocation and determine if this is a source of controversy.

6. Is management satisfied with the present marketing organization and methods of selling, or are significant changes being contemplated or underway? If changes are underway, would comparisons be unrealistic?

7. What has been the trend during the past four years for administrative expenses, both in terms of actual amounts and percentage of revenues? Determine the causes for any significant changes.

8. Can the total cost of the CEO be determined?

9. Are the costs of options included in administrative expenses?

10. Are there costs in administrative expenses that are perquisites for executives and totally unrelated to the operation of the business? If yes, how many would be retained if there was a change in the control of the business, and how many would be discontinued? What is the annual cost of these items?

11. If the business under study is owned or controlled by a parent company, identify management fees or other assessments charged by the parent company. If there are such fees, learn the amounts and how they are recorded in the financial statements. Identify the expenses that are for services performed and essential to the business. If ownership of the business changes hands, would all of these fees cease? Identify parent company services that would have to be replaced.

CHAPTER 42
Income Recognition and Backlog

PRIMARY ISSUES AND OBSERVATIONS

A. Historically, management that is intent on manipulating reported income frequently resorts to schemes involving receivables, inventory, income recognition, or any combination thereof. However, improper income recognition is the most common. Premature or delayed recording of sales are common techniques for temporarily influencing profits, but in some of the more egregious corporate scandals, fictitious sales were simply created. Often there are legitimate questions as to the causes of excessive income recognition. Human errors and sloppy policy decisions are explanations to pursue before concluding that blatant fraud exists. If any fraud is found, it is safe to assume there is more to discover, and terminating the due diligence investigation is the best option.

B. The amount of backlog of firm orders can be one of the better indicators of the level of business to be anticipated, but it must be carefully evaluated and conclusions not quickly drawn. Large backlogs do not necessarily translate into large profits if margins are low or anticipated gross profits emerge over a long period of time. Backlogs may only reflect a portion of a business's future revenues because of orders to be received, and if some sales are for cash. If all sales are for cash, as in retailing, there will be no backlog. Regardless, a large backlog with strong gross profit is a very healthy asset; on the other hand, a very weak backlog is a warning signal.

C. Fortunately, most businesses are managed on an ethical basis, so the emphasis in the investor's study is simply one of confirming methods of reporting income, recording backlog, and discerning the relevant procedures and policies of the seller.

QUESTIONS AND PROCEDURES

1. What are this business's policies and procedures for recognition of a firm order? What orders are booked and included in the backlog? When is an order an order? Is there any evidence of sales being booked prematurely or reversed?

2. Identify all sources of nonoperating income, such as interest, royalty payments, sales of assets, rental and investment income, etc. For each, determine the amount of income, probability of continuation, and when and if it will cease. Is there any indication of premature booking of this income?

3. What are this business's policies and procedures for removing delivered or cancelled orders from the backlog? Are partially completed orders accounted for under percentage of completion accounting reduced from the backlog during production?

4. Determine the percentage of sales produced from sold orders and those sold from inventory accumulated in anticipation of sales.

5. Does this business receive front-end cash, such as with installment sales, mobilization payments, subscription payments, membership fees, and down payments? How are these recorded?

6. What percentage of the sales are for cash? Is there any evidence of skimming or theft? Review for adequacy security procedures to prevent theft. Is this a serious problem area?

7. What is the present backlog by product or service line of unfilled orders? Is this backlog normal, high, low, increasing, or declining? Request copies of all internal backlog reports.

8. How much gross profit by product or service lines remains in the backlog? Calculate in which quarters the gross profit will be recognized.

9. What was the backlog six months and one year ago? Do seasonal factors affect the backlog?

10. Is production on engineered equipment started without a signed purchase order?

11. Is there any evidence that the backlog is inflated to present an optimistic picture?

12. Is there any evidence of cross sales with another business to inflate profits?

13. Is there any evidence of sales sold at or below cost to inflate revenues?

14. Have there been any unusual transactions or volume of transactions in the last days preceding the close of a quarter or fiscal year? If yes, identify the circumstances and impact upon reported income.

15. Does this business engage in any of the transactions listed below, or have a history of such transactions? If yes, determine how they are recorded on the financial statements, including backlog reports. From what points listed below are revenues, income, and losses recognized?

- Installment sales
- Customer rebates
- Returned goods
- Claims against customers
- Warranty claims
- Contracts subject to renegotiation
- Lease purchase revenues
- Franchise sales
- Revenues preceding associated costs
- Anticipated tax refunds
- Dispute or litigation settlements
- Retentions
- Partial shipments
- Cancelled orders

16. Have there been any sales of products or assets with agreements to repurchase? If yes, obtain complete details.

17. Does this business have a practice of paying "mark down" money, guaranteeing retailers an agreed level of profits? If yes, obtain full details, including the obligations outstanding.

18. Describe the procedures for recognizing revenues and income or losses when percentage of completed contracts accounting is used.

a) Describe in detail the method of taking up income. Obtain whatever forms or reports exist.

b) Describe the contingency reserves established for unknown variables.

c) Is there any profit "hold back" or deferred profit? If yes, when is it taken?

d) How reliable are the original cost estimates?

e) How reliable are estimates of percentage complete while jobs are in progress?

f) Is the "cost to complete" recalculated each month?

g) How are retentions recorded?

h) How well are change orders captured and recorded?

i) Are backlogs reduced as work is completed?

j) Review all present jobs in house. Describe their status as it regards completion, profits taken, and profit remaining. Identify any jobs that may be completed at a loss.

k) Overall, what has been the business's record for accuracy in estimating costs and percentage of completion as jobs progress? Compare the jobs completed during the past year with the original estimates of gross profit.

19. Does the business have a written or unwritten "bill and hold" policy determining when revenues may or may not be recorded and/or billed, although the product has not been shipped or a job is incomplete? If written, obtain a copy. What has been the business's practice?

20. Are orders and/or revenues recorded if the customer retains the right to cancel the order?

21. Identify any incidents and the circumstances under which the business has recorded revenues for products not shipped or services not performed.

CHAPTER 43
Intracompany Transactions

PRIMARY ISSUES AND OBSERVATIONS

A. Intracompany transactions have the potential to occur whenever a business has multiple business units, such as subsidiaries or divisions. The business under study may be the entire business, or one or more units controlled by the same parent. Transactions are not limited to product or service sales, but may encompass loans, investments, and transfers or training of personnel. The business philosophy of the parent company will ultimately influence the type and volume of transactions. Strong parent control may maximize the number of transactions and dictate the terms. Others may believe unit independence will produce the greatest profits and neither encourage or discourage intracompany transactions. Intracompany transactions may demonstrate real synergistic advantages, but they also may conceal improper business practices. Past failures to exploit the full potential of intracompany transactions may represent an added opportunity for an investor.

B. The accounting for all intracompany transactions must be reviewed in detail, although it may be complex and possibly intentionally opaque. Review the accounting methods and policies to learn if they reflect an intent to accurately record the income or losses of each business unit. Management fees, interest charges, arbitrary charges by the parent company, and transfer pricing may distort the true profitability of a business unit. Investigators in their financial review remember intracompany transactions, both real and fictitious, have been used by unethical management to enhance reported income.

C. The presence of any transfer pricing to reduce tax obligations constitutes a major area of concern requiring intense investigation.

Management may be reluctant to disclose the existence of transfer pricing because of possible civil or even criminal penalties if caught. If there are transactions of any type between foreign subsidiaries and domestic or foreign subsidiaries, a potential for transfer pricing exists.

QUESTIONS AND PROCEDURES

1. What are the operational and financial relationships between subsidiaries, divisions, joint ventures, partnerships, and any other internal profit centers? Identify and review all intracompany transactions for the past year and the amounts recorded on each balance sheet. Evaluate the role and philosophy of the parent in setting policy.

2. Describe, in detail, all types of intracompany sales and identify each account affected. What are the policies governing all intracompany sales? How is pricing determined, and what discretion is permitted? Are these sales mandated or optional? Is there any dissatisfaction with the price or quality of the products or services provided from a sister business?

3. Describe any transfer pricing designed to assign profits to one business unit over another. Does the business have defensible, written transfer pricing policies? If yes, request copies. Has any government or government agency questioned, investigated, or charged the business with transfer pricing?

4. Describe any management fees charged by the parent to subsidiaries or divisions. How are these calculated? What services does the parent provide to its subsidiaries or divisions? Are management fees a major source of controversy?

5. Are there any subsidiaries, joint ventures, or partnerships not actually engaged in operations through which financial transactions are routed? If yes, what is the purpose? Does the business have any subsidiaries located in countries known to be tax havens?

6. How does the parent extract cash from its operational units?

7. How does the parent provide cash to operating units? Are these treated as loans?

8. Are there any intracompany loans? If yes, determine the origin, purpose, and future plans for their retirement.

9. Are there any intracompany investments? If yes, determine the origin and present purpose.

10. Have there been any nonrecurring or unusual transactions between subsidiaries or affiliated companies?

11. What are the methods of moving cash between business units and the degree of financial independence of each? Are intracompany transactions

settled with cash transfers? Do operating units have their own bank accounts? What funds are deposited and disbursed from these accounts?

12. If cash is managed centrally, describe the system.

13. How does the parent collect cash from less than 100 percent–owned operations or investments, including joint ventures? Under what conditions are funds advanced to these businesses?

14. If the business being studied is acquired or divested, determine what services or products are provided by the parent or sister businesses that may have to be replaced.

15. Are there intracompany charges for use of intangibles, such as technology, rights to know-how, patents, marketing rights, customer lists, trademarks, and trade names? If yes, obtain full details, amounts involved, and copies of whatever documentation exists. Have any of these intangible assets been assigned to a nonoperating subsidiary? If yes, obtain full details.

16. Are there personnel transfers and/or promotion of personnel from one business unit to another? Is this an organized and encouraged activity?

CHAPTER 44
Real Estate

PRIMARY ISSUES AND OBSERVATIONS

A. The real estate owned or leased by the business should be systematically studied, parcel by parcel. Each parcel is unique and may have hidden value or unanticipated liabilities. If at all possible, every facility should be visited and inspected as to use, condition, and significant neighborhood factors. Old photographs can be misleading if taken in better days, prior to deterioration, or before additions were constructed. Appraisals must be viewed with a degree of skepticism because they are only opinions, and appraisers seem to have varying levels of integrity. Appraisals less than a year old prepared by competent professionals do have real value, but in all cases, two questions must be asked: who paid for the appraisal, and what was its purpose?

B. An overriding consideration in evaluating real estate is determining its importance to the day-to-day operations of the business. Just how essential any real estate property is to the business must be evaluated. Is critical property too small, menaced by periodic flooding, threatened with an imminent domain proceeding, or any other peril capable of causing a cessation of business?

C. Do any real estate parcels represent a significantly undervalued asset? Older businesses that acquired real estate years ago may have property that has greatly increased in value. The depreciated book value is often much lower than replacement and/or market values. Greatly increased market value of real estate is of interest, but of little use if the property is essential to the business and cannot be sold. If the property is in excess and can be sold, this is a means for an investor to recover a portion of his investment.

QUESTIONS AND PROCEDURES:

1. Who in this business is responsible for managing, buying, leasing, and selling real estate?
2. For all real estate owned or leased by the business, obtain the following information:

   a) Address and legal description, if available.
   b) Description and use of the facility. Take current photographs if possible.
   c) If owned, date of purchase, price paid, and cost of improvements.
   d) Estimate market value and current tax base or depreciated value. If sold, estimate the amount of depreciation recapture.
   e) If leased, the terms of the lease, expiration date, and possibility of renewal. Describe any lease hold improvements and their depreciated book value. Describe who is the landlord, and describe the relationship with the landlord. Would loss of the lease damage the business?
   f) Number of employees at the facility.
   g) Square feet of space under roof. Separate by office, warehouse, etc.
   h) Total acreage.
   i) Age of facility and general condition. Is there compliance with all applicable codes—fire, safety, provisions for the handicapped, structure, etc.? If not, estimate cost of compliance.
   j) Mortgages, if any, and the amounts remaining and monthly payments. Do the balances equal the amounts on the balance sheet?
   k) Known or suspected environmental problems. Request copies of all phase 1, 2, or 3 environmental studies.
   l) Does the business presently lease or sublease to others? Identify tenants and terms of the lease.
   m) What is the tax appraisal and annual "ad valorem" taxes? Has this appraisal been contested?
   n) Are property taxes current or delinquent?
   o) Are maintenance costs considered excessive? Are major repairs required?
   p) Estimate the difficulty in marketing the property if considered desirable or necessary.
   q) What insurance is carried? Is it adequate?
3. Is any of the real estate for sale? If yes, for how long, and what is the asking price?

4. Are negotiations in progress or contemplated near term to acquire or lease new facilities? If yes, what is the status of the negotiations?

5. Are new facilities under construction? If yes, why and how is the construction financed?

6. Are any facilities shut down, vacant, or only partially utilized? If yes, why, and what are the plans for the property?

7. Do shareholders, officers, or employees own any real estate or equipment leased by the business? If yes, describe in detail, including a comparison of rents paid vs. normal area market rents.

8. Does the business have a clear title to the property it believes it owns? Is there title insurance? Have there been property boundary surveys? Are there any property line disputes?

9. Does the business own mineral rights to all its property? Identify all leases for mineral rights. Determine the cost and estimated present value of the minerals.

10. Have any appraisals of company-owned or leased property been conducted within the past three years? If yes, why were they conducted? Obtain copies.

11. Are there any significant advantages or disadvantages the business experiences as a result of its facilities' locations? Are any in high-risk areas subject to thefts, vandalism, or riots?

12. Are present facilities adequate? If more are required, when? Can present facilities be expanded to accommodate growth? At what percentage of capacity does management believe the present business is operating with its existing facilities?

13. Are any of the properties located where they could be damaged by floods? Is there any record of flood damage? Are any in coastal areas subject to hurricanes?

14. Has any real estate been either bought from or sold to any shareholders, directors, or management executives within the past five years? If yes, obtain complete details.

15. Do any of the facilities constitute either a competitive advantage or disadvantage because of location, energy costs, freight costs, transportation access, hiring of employees, or other causes?

CHAPTER 45
Investment Questions and Issues

PRIMARY ISSUES AND OBSERVATIONS

There are critical questions that do not fit into any distinct category that are applicable if the study is part of a due diligence program prior to completing an acquisition. The response to any of these questions could reveal information not previously known, and some could result in modifying the contemplated transaction or constitute a "deal killer."

QUESTIONS AND PROCEDURES

1. Are there any third-party approvals necessary to complete this investment or acquisition?

2. Do the seller's negotiators have authority to close the transaction? Who will sign closing documents? Are all required signers willing to sign?

3. Is management's vision of the future for the business and the industry consistent with that of the investor? What earnings forecasts is the investor relying upon, and does the selling management agree that they are attainable?

4. How realistic are projections of synergy? Are there specific, detailed plans to obtain the synergy?

5. Identify any investment bankers, brokers, individuals, or financial advisors who have been retained by any party. What fees have they been paid, and what obligations exist to each? Are there any who may claim fees that are disputed and/or unauthorized?

6. Are there any individuals who may claim finder's fees although they are not formally retained? If yes, identify the circumstances.

7. Identify all consultants or consulting organizations and their role or assignments during the past two years. What have they been paid, and what continuing obligations exist?

8. Estimate the importance of any accountants, lawyers, investment bankers, or consultants who have a strong influence on either management or the owners. If the transaction is completed, will any lose a client, and is it possible their actions are being influenced by this fact? Identify those actively supporting the acquisition.

9. Have any formal valuations of the business been conducted? If yes, obtain copies and learn the purpose of the valuation. If the business has an ESOP plan, obtain copies of all valuations.

10. Have investment bankers or brokers prepared any valuations and pro forma financial projections for use in sales presentations? Do the sellers believe the projections and consider them a basis for pricing? Are the projections realistic, or fantasy?

11. Is it anticipated that "fairness opinion" letters will be required? Who will prepare such letters, and what will be the cost?

12. Will insurance be required to guarantee the integrity of the financial statements and other warranties and representations? Will insurance or derivative contracts be required to protect against credit risks?

13. Identify and describe sales of businesses, including prices paid within the past three years that are comparable to this business or in the industry. Are these sales influencing the price negotiations?

14. Identify any public companies comparable to this one and the latest book values, return on equity, earnings, PE ratio, and market price per share.

15. Have any written reports or studies of the business, industry, markets, or specific problems been prepared by professionals or analysts in the past three years? If yes, obtain copies?

16. What is the general business climate in the states, countries, and communities in which this business is located? How do these locations compare with competitors?

17. Identify trade associations or societies of which this business is a member. Are there important industry trade associations or societies of which this business is not a member? Are there major trade shows in which this business does not participate?

18. Has the investor planned any changes for the business?

19. In the selling management's opinion, what probable good or bad events are likely to occur that could materially affect the business?

20. If the transaction contemplated is an acquisition of assets and selected liabilities, are the tax effects of depreciation recapture by the seller understood?

21. What is the source of the buyer's financing?

22. Do all parties to the transaction understand the warranties and representations that will be expected?

CHAPTER 46
Off–Balance Sheet Items

PRIMARY ISSUES AND OBSERVATIONS:

A. Many of the most important aspects of a business are not reflected on the balance sheet. Reliance solely on financial statements and interviews with a limited number of owners or executives will only result in a cursory understanding of the business. However, during an in-depth due diligence investigation, perceptive investigators should acquire sufficient insight to recognize off-balance assets and make value judgments. Precise financial estimates may be impossible, but three subjective categories are quite possible: high value, negative value, and neutral. A going business has a name, reputation, assembled workforce, and established relationships that make it possible to function and continue. None of these appear on the balance sheet, yet each one is essential to the business and should be evaluated.

Perhaps the most valuable asset of a business not reflected on its balance sheet is the management and employees. Building a workforce with all the necessary skills to function as a team is a very long, expensive process. Creating the systems, relationships, and culture in which the employees can efficiently perform evolves over a long period of time. For most established businesses, the cost of assembling a comparable workforce and organizing it into a functioning team would be staggering, if not impossible.

B. A search for other assets, liabilities, and related entities not reflected on the balance sheet may result in the discovery of issues and relationships that have the potential to greatly modify an investor's position. Complicating the search for off–balance sheet items may be the absence of a paper trail, and their existence will only become known through employee disclosures. These entities and relationships are usually legitimate, but their purpose and financial effect upon the business requires close study. Entities created through complex financial engineering should receive particular attention. The discovery of one questionable off–balance sheet item should alert investigators to the probability that there are others, and that the business has a propensity for their creation.

C. There clearly are two distinct types of off–balance sheet items as described above. One is associated with the accumulated character and nature of the business, and the others are to benefit the business and/or individuals financially. If there are improprieties, they are likely to be found in the latter category. If suspected, a first step is to identify the executive most likely to have information.

QUESTIONS AND PROCEDURES

1. How well known and important for the business is its name? Is it best known for its legal name or some other name? Is the name a valuable asset? If the name was changed, would this be a major problem?

2. What is the reputation of the business with investors, employees, customers, and the communities in which it is located?

3. What is the composition of the workforce? What are its special skills? How is it unique?

4. Does this business have a history of creating off–balance sheet entities with the purpose of influencing reported earnings or to conceal other activities? Identify all such entities, the purpose of each, their location, and present activity. Identify the executives involved in their creation and/or administration.

5. If there are off–balance sheet entities, identify the attorneys, accountants, and financial institutions involved in their creation. Is there any question as to the legality of the entities?

6. Are there any offshore subsidiaries, minority investments in financial institutions, offices, agents, or other entities where the purpose is primarily financial and not operational? Identify all foreign commission agents and the amounts they have been paid in the past two years.

7. Identify any partnerships, joint ventures, or businesses in which any shareholder, director, or officer has a financial interest in which the business conducts business or has been involved in financial transactions. Are any of these entities offshore? For each of these relationships, determine the annual volume of transactions in purchases or sales. When compared to alternatives, has the relationship benefited the business?

8. Conduct a search for positive off–balance sheet assets, such as rebates, favorable long-term contracts, a backlog, advantageous close relations with customers or vendors, etc.

9. Review all leases to determine if they are properly recorded and if the complete obligation is known.

10. Review compensation agreements or employment contracts for termination payments or any continuing obligations after termination.

11. Accumulate a list of all assets and liabilities identified during the due diligence investigation that are not on the last balance sheet but are normal for an ongoing business, as well as purchase contracts, letters of credit, performance guarantees, etc.

12. Has the business or any executive of the business made written or oral commitments to purchase or repurchase assets once owned by the business or any shareholder or officer?

CHAPTER 47
Assets and Liabilities Excluded

PRIMARY ISSUES AND OBSERVATIONS

A. If the due diligence investigation is intended as a prelude to an acquisition or merger, it is appropriate to look for assets and/or liabilities that should or can be excluded from the transaction. If the transaction is to be structured as an "asset deal" in which shares are not purchased but selected assets, liabilities, and the going business are acquired, then identification of precisely what is being acquired takes on added importance. The lists in this chapter are intended only as a reminder of common possibilities. They are by no means all-inclusive, and transactions can usually be structured to exclude any assets or liabilities the parties agree upon.

When the business to be acquired is less than a complete stand-alone business, such as a joint venture, division or product line, identification of the functions excluded and the cost of their replacement becomes a task for the due diligence investigators. Planning for replacement of the functions should be complete prior to closing to enable the business to continue without disruption. The lists of functions commonly provided by the seller that may be excluded in the transaction are listed at the conclusion of this chapter.

B. While there may be many reasons for excluding assets, there are three primary reasons: to reduce the assets purchased and consequently reduce the purchase price, because of the uncertain value of an asset, and because the assets are dear to the seller. The primary reason for excluding liabilities is uncertainty as to financial exposure, debt associated with an excluded asset, and a buyer being simply unwilling to assume the liability. Liabilities may prove difficult to avoid because of legal complications, existing guarantors, and provisions of bulk sales laws.

C. Some assets a seller wishes to retain may have importance all out of proportion to their book or actual monetary value. These usually are personal items, such as club memberships, automobiles, artwork, tickets to sporting events, water- or aircraft, and hunting and fishing camps. Usually, the buyer has little interest in retaining these assets, but should never underestimate their importance to the seller.

ASSETS FOR EXCLUSION

1. The following is a list of assets commonly considered for deletion in transactions. Do they exist, and should they be excluded?

   a) Real estate

   b) Investments unrelated to the primary business

   c) Personal automobiles

   d) Key-person life insurance

   e) Airplanes

   f) Boats

   g) Hunting lodges owned or leased

   h) Fishing camps owned or leased

   i) Personal residences

   j) Tickets to sporting events

   k) Artwork

   l) Patents or licenses

   m) Club memberships

   n) Professional and trade organization memberships

   o) Litigation against others

   p) Tax refunds

   q) Controversial receivables

   r) Loans to shareholders, officers, or employees

   s) Insurance settlements

LIABILITIES FOR EXCLUSION

2. This is a list of liabilities frequently considered for exclusion. Do they exist, and are they candidates for exclusion?

a) Liabilities associated with any excluded assets

b) Outstanding litigation against the business

c) Environmental issues unknown or not evaluated

d) Cost of environmental remedial action

e) Obligations guaranteed by officers or shareholders

f) Any indebtedness primarily incurred for the personal benefit of shareholders or officers.

g) Unresolved warranty claims and/or disputes with customers

h) Pension liability

i) Vacation and sick pay

j) Deferred compensation

k) Termination pay

l) Compensation to injured or disabled employees

m) Stock repurchase obligations

FUNCTIONS EXCLUDED

3. If the business under study is anything other than a complete stand-alone business, and essential services are provided by a parent or sister company, then the excluded services must be identified and their replacements planned. The list is of common functions that may be excluded.

a) Accounting services

b) Treasury and banking services

c) Cash management

d) Marketing of products or services

e) Market research

f) Technology support

g) Insurance

h) Management oversight

i) Legal services

j) Advantageous vendor contracts

k) Name of business, and brand names

l) Advertising

CHAPTER 48

Financial Ratios and Trends

PRIMARY ISSUES AND OBSERVATIONS

A. The results of ratios are symptoms that can lead to the identification of favorable or alarming causes, but conclusions should not be drawn exclusively from ratios. Comparisons with industry or competitor ratios can be misleading because of a lack of uniformity in accounting systems and the difficulty of obtaining accurate information. Perhaps most misleading of all are comparisons with unrelated and different businesses. A ratio for a business may appear excellent or unsatisfactory when compared to totally different businesses in other industries.

Financial ratios may readily confirm alarming conditions, such as a negative current ratio or a low percentage of gross profit, but cash flow problems and a lack of profitability are almost certainly well known and no surprise. They also may identify marginal conditions requiring further study.

B. Industry statistics and ratios play a critical role in evaluating businesses through comparisons with competitors. These ratios are important indicators of performance and efficiency and have influenced the careers of many CEOs. The most important in many industries is market share, which is simply the percentage of the market a business enjoys. Other statistics are costs of unit production measured in terms common to the industry, such as tons, cases, miles, man-hours, etc. A chronic problem persists in that industry data usually is submitted on an honor system basis and is not readily verified. Further distortion occurs when not all industry members participate. Regardless, industry statistics are invaluable information usually obtainable from the business under study and/or trade associations or trade magazines.

C. Ratios are of greatest value to identify trends within a business or industry. Historical industry data will have to be obtained. Prior financial statements must be reviewed to ascertain that no significant changes in accounting policies occurred during the periods under study. Positive and negative trends are usually well known without calculating trends, but the trends will indicate the magnitude and velocity of the changes.

Note: There are a substantial number of financial ratios available and in use, but a few are most common and valuable. However, some executives have exotic favorites they will insist upon. There always are the practical considerations of time constraints in any business investigation and the need to separate what one needs to know from what would be nice to know.

RATIOS

1. Identify and calculate the common industry statistics and ratios applicable to this business. How does this business compare or rank?

2. Current ratio. Current assets divided by current liabilities is an indication of liquidity. For businesses affected by seasonal factors, the results may be misleading.

3. Gross profit margin percentage. The gross profit divided by sales revenues indicates the profit margins being experienced. Trends may indicate increased or declining costs, and/or changes in pricing, or both. Significant changes require priority study.

4. Earnings percentage. The pretax earnings divided by revenues and the after-tax earnings divided by revenues indicates the level of profitability in relation to total revenues.

5. Equity return. After-tax earnings divided by total shareholder equity indicates the percentage of return the shareholders are experiencing on the investment and may be useful in comparison to alternative investments.

6. Earnings per common share. The total after-tax earnings divided by the number of common shares outstanding indicates the earnings per share. Caution must be exercised in this calculation because of the possibility of classes of common, treatment of stock options, and other obligations that could affect the return to stockholders.

7. Other ratios may be calculated based on the interest and needs of the investor. These may include:

a) Debt to equity
b) Sales to total assets
c) Net income to total assets
d) Taxes paid to total income
e) Administrative costs to total revenues
f) Selling expense to revenues
g) Cost per unit sold

CHAPTER 49
Warning Signs

There are events, conditions, and activities that constitute warnings, and their presence warrants even more diligent study and investigation. Often, the warnings are easily explained or only reflect a style of conducting business, but they may also signal deeper problems. The list given below is meant to provide the reader with some common warning signs to look out for.

WARNING SIGNS

1. The sellers insist on selling on a "where is, as is" basis.
2. There are unreasonable restrictions placed upon the due diligence process.
3. There has been the unexpected departure of a key executive.
4. The CEO prides himself on being an innovator and risk taker.
5. The products or services the business touts to become a major portion of the business in five years are presently small and/or unproven.
6. The CEO is evasive with shareholders, analysts, or others seeking information about the business.
7. Annual meetings are conducted in remote locations, of short duration, scripted, and with little or no opportunity for questions.
8. Ratings by financial institutions are declining.
9. A high level of secretiveness regarding financial information and projections exists. Are employees in nonpublic companies apprised of the financial condition?
10. Financial statements are inconsistent and do not support public pronouncements.

11. Financial statements are complex, with voluminous notes not readily understood.

12. Annual and quarterly earnings have been erratic.

13. Annual and quarterly financial reports show consistent unbroken increases in earnings.

14. The business has numerous subsidiaries or divisions and a management philosophy of loose and decentralized control.

15. There have been significant changes in accounting policies and/or a change of auditors. The business has adjusted prior financial reports.

16. The business has not recognized or adjusted to major industry changes.

17. Analysts have issued "sell" opinions.

18. Credit reports indicate the business is slow to pay its bills.

19. Rating agencies have low or downgraded ratings of the business.

20. Bloggers are critical of the business.

21. The business has an active PR program touting the CEO. The business is in a high-flying glamorous industry.

22. There are substantial onetime events enhancing earnings.

23. Large reserves have been established to cover the cost of restructuring and discontinued operations.

24. The board of directors rarely meets and/or is totally controlled by the CEO.

25. There has been a substantial volume of insider trading.

26. The backlog of unfilled orders is declining.

27. Executives have received excessive compensation inconsistent with the performance of the business.

28. Key shareholders, directors, or executives have been associated with businesses that failed during their involvement with the business.

CHAPTER 50
Outrageous Improprieties

The need for aggressive due diligence can be best illustrated by reviewing a very incomplete and partial list of outrageous improprieties occurring within the past 10 years. In most cases, they escaped detection for years, and the executives involved prior to their outing were admired business leaders, often praised in the business media. Investors, auditors, directors, most employees, and their communities were all deceived. Many of the schemes were original or brazen, extreme variations of earlier improper practices, but all constitute a warning to present-day investigators to be wary and alert. Yet it is safe to assume that somewhere today, there are managements engaged in old or new devious schemes for their enrichment. **Never underestimate greed.**

OUTRAGEOUS IMPROPRIETIES

1. Revision of stock option terms when stock declines in value, and "spring loading" before announcing good news. (Over 100 companies were being investigated in 2007.)
2. Off-balance sheet partnerships used to conceal debt and/or inflate income (Enron).
3. Cross-sales schemes in which two companies would agree to sell each other's assets at inflated prices (Global Crossing).
4. Writing up the value of old assets (Waste Management).
5. Depreciation manipulation to underdepreciate and enhance income (Waste Management).

6. Executive loans granted to executives with no realistic expectations that they will ever be repaid, or repaid with inflated stock (WorldCom, Tyco, Adelphia).

7. Derivatives used to conceal debt or inflate income (Enron).

8. Mark-to-market accounting, now outlawed, used to prematurely recognize income that may or may not happen (Enron, Dynegy, and other energy traders).

9. Capitalizing expenses by recording operating expenses as capital assets (WorldCom).

10. Acquisition accounting used to inflate income (HealthSouth, Tyco).

11. Premature claim recognition in which claims or litigation against others are recorded as income although the issues are not resolved (Halliburton).

12. Round-trip trades are trades between two independent companies designed to inflate revenues and make the businesses appear larger (Dynegy).

13. Technology advances claims that are premature or false (Imclone).

14. Purchase of personal assets with corporate funds and recording the purchase as a business expense (Tyco).

15. Volume discounts recorded as income (Fleming).

16. "Points of sale" agreements in which manufacturers pay wholesalers to market their products and inflate rebates (Royal Ahold).

17. "Pump and dump" schemes using glowing, inaccurate, exaggerated, or premature press releases to inflate the value of the stock (Rocky Mountain Energy Corp.).

18. Fraud on a scale so large and brazen, few suspected it (WorldCom, Enron, HealthSouth, Global Crossing, etc.).

Index

accounting: accounting general
questions, 135–37; accounting
policies, 139–42; accounts and
notes receivable, 143–45; cost of
sales and gross profit, 163–64;
fixed and other assets, 155–58;
income recognition and backlog,
167–70; intracompany
transactions, 171–73; inventory,
151–54; liabilities, 159–61; real
estate, 175–77; selling and
general and administrative
expenses (SG&A), 165–66; taxes,
147–49
accounting policies, 139–42; assets
and, 155; "bill and hold," 170;
financial ratios and, 191, 192;
mark-to-market, 198; percentage
of completed contracts, 169;
transfer pricing and, 171
accounting system, 31–32, 135–37
accounts and notes receivable,
143–45
accounts payable, 159–61

acquisition, 3, 14, 96, 161; business
culture and, 89
administrative costs, 85, 165–66
advertising, 55–56, 58
alarms, key issues and, 11–15
anti-takeover defenses, 15
appraisal, real estate, 175
assets, 127–28, 155–58; accounts
receivable and, 143; divestment
of, 15, 21; intangible, 47, 155, 157,
173; liabilities excluded and, 187–
89; off–balance sheet items, 183–
85; real estate, 175–77
audit and auditors, 101, 131, 136,
137; tax, 147, 148

backlog of orders, 64, 167–70
banks and financial institutions,
123–25
benefit plans, 81–84, 86
"bill and hold" policy, 170
boards of directors, 21–23
bonding, 115–17
bribes and kickbacks, 50, 69, 96

budgets, 111–12, 114
business culture, 89–92, 100
business philosophy, 171
business practices, 3

capital structure, 17–20
cash and cash management, 131–33
cash flow, 14, 123, 191
cash sales, 167
CEO (chief executive officer), 22, 28,
    195, 196; business policies of, 26,
    27; expenses of, 165, 166;
    management philosophy of, 89;
    planning and, 113, 114
charitable contributions, 91–92
chief executive officer. See CEO
commission payments, 84
commodity prices, 68, 129
compatibility, 25–26
compensation, 25, 26; for directors,
    21, 22; employee benefits and,
    81–84; for executives, 13; for key
    employees, 27
compensation agreements, 48
compensation committee, 23
competence, 25–26
competition, 43–45, 61–62;
    employee compensation and, 81,
    82; pricing and, 52; taxes and, 147
competitive bids, 99
confidence, 139
confidential information
    agreements, 2, 3, 5, 72
conflicts of interest, 28
constraints, 1, 3, 12
Consumer Product Safety
    Commission, 95
continuity, 25, 26
contracts, 1; government, 48, 99–
    103; information systems, 107
contract employees, 71, 72
cost-benefit analysis, 105, 107
cost of sales, 163–64
costs, 12; ability to absorb, 85;
    compensation and, 81;

environmental remediation, 119,
    120; freight and transport, 64, 69;
    legal, 94; marketing, 47; pricing
    and, 52, 53; taxes, 147–49; of unit
    production, 191. See also
    expenditures
credit, 123–25, 128, 132
cross-sales schemes, 197
culture, business, 89–92, 100
current ratio, 192. See also financial
    ratios and trends
customers: accounts receivable and,
    143–45; markets and, 39–41;
    pricing and, 53

debt, 13, 19, 159; credit and, 123–25,
    128, 132
decision making, 21, 28
depreciation, 156, 197
derivatives, 13, 127–28, 130, 198. See
    also hedge funds
dilemma, 1
directors, 21–23
divestment, 15, 21
dividend policy, 19
document evaluation, 2–3
document gathering, 8
due diligence, getting started on.
    See planning due diligence

earnings percentage, 192
earnings per common share, 192
elected officials, 100, 102. See also
    political influence
employees, 71–75; as business asset,
    183; business culture and, 89;
    compensation and benefits, 81–
    84; politics and, 103; retirement
    plans, 73, 85–87 (see also
    retirement plans); stock option
    plans (ESOP), 19, 83, 85, 87, 180;
    temporary, 71, 72; training
    programs for, 73
employee issues: culture of the
    business, 89–92; employee

compensation and benefits,
81–84; human resources and
employees, 71–75; retirement
plans, 401(k)s, and ESOPs, 85–87;
union issues, 77–79
employment contracts, 83
environmental issues, 119–22;
hazardous materials and, 121–22
equity return, 192
ESOP plan, 19, 83, 85, 87, 180
excluded assets and liabilities,
187–89
executives, 196; accounting policy
and, 139; acquisition and, 3;
compensation for, 13, 27;
competitive markets and, 43;
loans to, 198; planning and, 114.
See also CEO
expenditures, 12, 14, 47;
administrative, 165–66;
advertising, 55–56; budget and,
111–12, 114; manufacturing, 62.
See also costs

fidelity bonds, 115
finance: cash and cash
management, 131–33; debt,
banks, and financial institutions,
123–25; investments, hedging,
and derivatives, 127–30
finance contracts, 50
financial forecasts, 13
financial institutions, 123–25
financial ratios and trends, 191–93
financial responsibility, 119
financial statements, 4, 31, 130, 192,
196; accounting and, 135–37, 139;
assets and, 157; assets in, 155;
backlog reports in, 169; budget
and, 111; liabilities in, 160;
reliance on, 12
fixed assets, 155–58
forward contracts, 34
401(k) plans, 83, 85, 86, 129. *See also*
retirement plans

freight and transport costs, 64, 69
functions excluded, 189

globalization, 13, 61
governance, 21–23
government agencies, 148
government contracts, 48, 99–103
government regulations, 93–97, 103;
environmental remediation, 119,
120, 122
gross profit margin percentage, 192
gross profits, 32, 163–64, 167, 168

hazardous materials, 121–22. *See
also* environmental issues
health hazards, 73
health insurance, 116
hedge funds, 13, 127, 129
human resources, 71–75. *See also*
employees

identifying and creating products
and services: products and
services, 31–34; R&D and
technology, 35–38
illegal workers, 73
incentive plans, 27
income, 14–15, 31; accounting
policy and, 141–42; inventory
and, 151; liabilities and, 159;
nonoperating, 168; recognition
and backlog, 167–70
incorporation, 18
information systems, 105–8;
Internet, 109–10
insurance and bonding, 115–17
insurance benefits, 82
intangible assets, 47, 155, 157, 173
intellectual property, 157
interest rates, 123
Internal Revenue Service (IRS),
148
Internet. *See* information systems
intracompany transactions, 4,
171–73

inventory systems, 64, 151–54
investment: hedging and
    derivatives, 127–30; questions
    and issues, 179–81; R&D, 35; risk
    in, 127–28; short-term, 131
investment decisions, 85
investor, 1, 2, 3, 31; preliminary
    agreement and, 7
investor relations, 57–59
IT. *See* information systems

joint ventures, 23, 187
judgment decision, 1
"just in time" systems, 65, 68, 152

key employees, 27. *See also*
    management
key issues and alarms, 11–15
kickbacks and bribes, 50, 69, 96

labor costs, 71. *See also* wage costs
labor relations, 77–79. *See also*
    employees
legal and government matters:
    government business, lobbying,
    and politics, 99–103; legal and
    regulatory issues, 93–97
legal structure, 17, 18
liabilities, 59–61, 119; excluded,
    187–89. *See also* debt
license agreements, 37, 106
litigation, 14, 93, 95, 147. *See also*
    legal and regulatory issues
loans, 123–25, 128, 129, 172, 198. *See
    also* debt

management, 12, 25–29; accounting
    and, 139; accounts receivable
    and, 143; administrative
    expenses and, 165; advertising
    and, 55; budget and, 111; as
    business asset, 183; of cash, 131–
    33; information systems and, 106;
    insurance and, 115; intangible
    assets and, 155; inventory and,

151–52, 153, 154; legislation and,
    94; manufacturing, 62, 64;
    marketing and, 47; perquisites
    for, 28–29; planning and, 113;
    politics and, 102; of product line,
    32; unions and, 77, 78. *See also*
    CEO; executives
management fees, 166
management philosophy, 89–90, 93
manufacturing, 61–65
mark down money, 53
markets and marketing, 47–50;
    advertising, 55–56; competition,
    43–45; markets and customers,
    39–41; marketing, selling, and
    distribution, 47–50; pricing, 51–
    53; public and investor relations,
    57–59
market value, 155, 157

negotiations, 3, 7; authority of, 17;
    union contracts, 78
nepotism, 28, 74
noncompetition agreements, 72

occupational health hazards, 73
off–balance sheet items, 183–85
officers: compensation for, 27;
    selection of, 28. *See also* CEO;
    directors
operational issues: budgets, 111–12;
    environmental and safety issues,
    119–22; information systems,
    105–8; insurance and bonding,
    115–17; Internet, 109–10;
    planning, 113–14
order backlogs, 64, 67–70
organizational structure, 31–32
organized labor, 77–79
outrageous improprieties, 197–98
outsourcing, 67–70
owners and managers: directors
    and governance, 21–23;
    management, 25–29; ownership
    and capital structure, 17–20

ownership, 113, 166; capital structure and, 17–20; performance bonds and, 115. *See also* shareholders

partnership, 17, 20, 23
payable accounts (liabilities), 159–61
payoffs, 96. *See also* kickbacks and bribes
performance bonds, 115, 116
performance review, 74
perquisites, for management, 28–29
personnel management, 25. *See also* employees
planning, 113–14
planning due diligence: basic information, getting started, 1–5; key issues and alarms, 11–15; preliminary critical information, 7–9
"points of sale" agreements, 198
political activity, 90
political influence, 99–103
PR. *See* public relations
preliminary critical information, 7–9
price-fixing, 96
pricing, 51–53, 68, 151; transfer, 149, 171–73
producing the products: manufacturing, 61–65; purchasing and outsourcing, 67–70
products and services, 31–34
profitability, 43, 47, 61; gross profits, 32, 163–64, 167, 168, 192; pricing and, 51; of product lines, 32; purchasing and, 67
profit-sharing plans, 83
promotion, 75
properties, 175–77
public information, 8
public relations (PR), 57–59

"pump and dump" schemes, 198
purchasing and outsourcing, 67–70

quality control, 63

R&D. *See* research and development
real estate, 175–77
receivable accounts, 143–45
regulatory issues, 93–97. *See also* government regulations
research and development (R&D), 35–38
resource deployment, 1
resource reserves, 158
retention, accounting for, 145
retirement plans, 73, 79, 82, 85–87; 401(k), 83, 85, 86, 129
revenues, 31, 61
round trip trades, 198

safety issues, 119–22
safety record, 73
sales and distribution, 47–50
costs of, 163–64. *See also* seller; selling
sales personnel, 49–50
Sarbanes-Oxley Act, 97, 136, 140
secrecy agreements, 2, 3, 5, 195
securities, 18, 19, 127
security concerns, 74, 106, 110, 158
seller: assets and, 155; financial report of, 12; investor and, 3; management of, 25
seller information, 2
selling: general and administrative (G&A) expenses and, 165–66. *See also* sales
services and products, 31–34
shareholders, 17, 18, 19–20, 192; government contracts and, 102; meetings of, 23
shipments, 65
skepticism, 7
sole proprietorships, 21

stock activity, 18, 19
stock option plans, 20; ESOP, 19, 83, 85, 87, 180. *See also* shareholders
subcontracting, 67, 70, 100
subsidies, 99

taxes, 147–49
technology, R&D, 35–38
telecommunications systems, 107; Internet, 109–10
temporary employees, 71, 72
time constraints, 12
toxic waste, 121. *See also* environmental issues
training programs, 73
transaction and evaluation issues: assets and liabilities excluded, 187–89; financial ratios and trends, 191–93; investments questions and issues, 179–81; off-balance sheet items, 183–85; outrageous improprieties, 197–98; warning signs, 195–96
transfer pricing, 149, 171–73
transport costs, 64, 69
trust funds, 86–87

union contracts, 78
union issues, 77–79

vendor relations, 68, 69–70. *See also* purchasing and outsourcing

wage costs, 63, 82. *See also* compensation
warning signs, 195–96
warranties, 33–34

ABOUT THE AUTHOR

GORDON BING is a Houston-based independent consultant specializing in multimillion dollar acquisitions and mergers in a wide variety of industries. He is the author of numerous books, including *Corporate Divestment, Corporate Acquisitions, Due Diligence Techniques and Analysis* (Quorum, 1996), and *Selecting Your Employer* (Butterworth-Heinemann, 2006).